CHINESE SPADE MONEY—*Created around 700 B.C., these coins were made of bronze in the shape of a spade and were used to represent the actual spades which till then had been a form of currency.*

CHARON'S OBOL—*The ancient Greeks placed this small silver coin into the mouth of a dead person to pay his ferry fare across the River Styx to the netherworld.*

TREE MONEY—*This was an early coin used in the American colonies which bore the symbol of either the oak, pine, or willow in order to make counterfeiting difficult.*

These are just a few of the wide range of coins you will encounter in this fascinating and comprehensive guide. Whether you collect ancient coins or modern, United States coins or foreign ones, you will find a wealth of valuable information in

COLLECTING COINS

DAVID HENDIN is the executive editor of United Feature Syndicate and Newspaper Enterprise Association, the nation's largest newspaper syndicate and feature service. He has been collecting coins since his childhood, in recent years specializing in ancient coins. He is a frequent lecturer to numismatic societies and is a regular columnist for *The Shekel*, magazine of the American Israel Numismatic Association. He is author of *Guide to Ancient Jewish Coins* and nine other books.

SIGNET Books on Games and Hobbies

COLLECTING COINS

by

David Hendin

A SIGNET BOOK

NEW AMERICAN LIBRARY

TIMES MIRROR

For my fellow collectors:

Ron, Mark, and Roy Hendin

NAL BOOKS ARE ALSO AVAILABLE AT DISCOUNTS IN BULK QUANTITY FOR
INDUSTRIAL OR SALES—PROMOTIONAL USE, FOR DETAILS, WRITE TO
PREMIUM MARKETING DIVISION, NEW AMERICAN LIBRARY, INC., 1301
AVENUE OF THE AMERICAS, NEW YORK, NEW YORK 10019.

SIGNET TRADEMARK REG. U.S. PAT. OFF. AND FOREIGN COUNTRIES
REGISTERED TRADEMARK—MARCA REGISTRADA
HECHO EN CHICAGO, U.S.A.

SIGNET, SIGNET CLASSICS, MENTOR, PLUME and MERIDIAN BOOKS
are published by The New American Library, Inc.,
1301 Avenue of the Americas, New York, New York 10019

First Signet Printing, December, 1978

1 2 3 4 5 6 7 8 9

PRINTED IN THE UNITED STATES OF AMERICA

Contents

Acknowledgements

The author gratefully acknowledges the following individuals, whose assistance was instrumental in completing this book: Morris Bram, Leo Dardarian, L.G. Davenport, George Gilbert, Dr. Aaron Hendin, Sandra Hendin, Harvey Hoffer, Ed Janis, Godfrey Kaye, Herb Kreindler, Dr. Yaakov Meshorer, Dr. Ira Rezak, Joe Rose, Phil Steiner, Fred Werner.

The material in Chapter 9 on ancient coin grades is reprinted from *The Illustrated Grading Guide to Ancient Numismatics* by Raymond Ladd (JSD Publications). By permission.

Photographs were supplied by American Israel Numismatic Association, American Numismatic Society, Amphora Coins, Chase Manhattan Bank, Collection of David Hendin, Harmer Rooke Numismatics, Superior Coin and Stamp Co., and Western Publishing Company.

1. Why Collect Coins?

Small Is Beautiful

The motto of the American Numismatic Society is *Parva ne pereant*, Latin for "Let small things not perish."

That is an excellent motto for the casual coin collector as well as the scholarly numismatist, for many coins are among the world's most beautiful and interesting small things. Coins are very tiny indeed when compared to other works of art. Only certain ancient carved gemstones and, perhaps, the ancient Egyptian scarabs and amulets are as small, yet as magnificently detailed, as coins.

In fact, coins are so small and compact in their beauty, it is in many ways a wonder that the hobby of coin collecting has become so popular the world around. An estimated five to ten million Americans collect coins, and there are countless millions more collectors around the world. Perhaps coin collecting is so popular today because of man's natural instinct as a hunter!

Most of us don't hunt animals any more. But a coin collector can easily experience the thrill of the chase while pursuing—sometimes for many years—a particular coin.

When a person collects coins he or she is also building a collection of art in miniature. Some of the portraits and scenes on coins and medals, both modern and ancient, can truly be considered masterpieces.

This is not a recent realization. There is nothing new about coin collecting. As long as 2,000 years ago wealthy Romans collected the Greek coins that were 200 to 300 years old even then. Indeed, the Roman emperor Augustus, who reigned from 27 B.C. to 14 A.D., was said to have owned a coin cabinet in which he built a fascinating collection. He even tried to spread his hobby around. On certain festivals he distributed, among other precious items, old foreign coins with portraits of ancient kings.

During the reign of Hadrian (117 to 138 A.D.), many wealthy and educated Romans collected the artistic coins of Greece, particularly those depicting scenes evoking the classical ideals of the day.

Hadrian

Medieval times brought a decline in coin collecting. The Dark Ages were unhealthy years for many of the arts and sciences we know today. However, the emperor Charlemagne (742–814 A.D.) was said to have built a coin collection, and a few European monasteries supposedly started collections of unusual kinds of money.

The Renaissance was a rebirth of many interests, among them the coin-collecting hobby. During the 1400s many artifacts of ancient Greece and Rome were dug up in Italy and surrounding areas. These discoveries, which included coins, led to new interest in the ancient arts. Many of the Italian artists of the day began to imitate the ancient coins. Today many of those Italian imitations—particularly of large Roman bronze coins—still exist and are recognized as objects of art and numismatic interest in their own right. They are referred to as "Paduans," since the famous engraver Giovanni Cavino (1500–1570), who began the practice of making them, lived in the city of Padua.

A Matter of Prestige

The interest in collecting beautiful coins spread along with revived interest in other areas of classical study throughout France and the rest of Central Europe. Within a few hundred years coin collecting had become a prestigious activity among various dignitaries and members of royal families, and coin collections had become something wonderful about which to boast. One reference notes that some of these avid collectors went so far as to "secretly have counterfeiters invent nonexistent rulers for them, so they would surely outdo their friends." These collectors forgot—or perhaps never realized—that they were ignoring the first requirement of numismatics: authenticity.

In those days, coin collecting was mainly limited to the person of some means. The common man was often uneducated, and at any rate had little time or interest in pursuing something as obscure as collecting tiny pieces of metal that other civilizations had used as money.

Gradually the rather specialized interest of collecting ancient coins began to expand. Many wars caused troops and citizens to move across borders with increasing regularity, and each person usually carried some of the money which was used in his home region. Thus strange and interesting coins began to be spread across the Continent and the world. This led to a more generalized interest in collecting various coins, and collectors began to specialize in "ancient coins," "foreign coins," "medieval coins," and even "oriental coins."

In the 1500s, books and pamphlets began to be published on coin collecting, and as interests continued to grow and broaden, so did the publications. In my library is a fascinating volume "Printed for R. Knaplock, at the Bishop's-Head in St. Paul's Churchyard. 1721." The title of the book is *An Inquirey Into the State of the Ancient Measures, the Attick, the Roman, and Especially the Jewish. With an Appendix, concerning our old English Money and Measures of Content.*

AN

INQUIRY

INTO THE

STATE

OF THE

Ancient Measures,

THE

ATTICK, the ROMAN,

And especially the

JEWISH.

WITH

An APPENDIX,

Concerning our old *English Money*,
and Measures of *Content*.

LONDON:

Printed for R. KNAPLOCK, at the *Bishop's-
Head* in St. *Paul's Church-yard.* 1721.

Of course the measures of content were linked to the ancient
monetary systems, since, as we will soon see, coinage began as a
simple way of guaranteeing the weight of pieces of precious
metals.

By the late nineteenth and early twentieth centuries, numismatics had become a full-fledged field of scholarly study. Indeed, nu-

mismatics today is a science in its own right, and reflects mightily on the related fields of history, archaeology, art, and economics.

Copied from Antiquity

For more than 2,000 years, coins of the realm have been patterned after coins issued by previous or different civilizations. Various Roman emperors issued "restitution" coins of earlier emperors which copied the inscription and design of the originals, adding only the inscription "REST[ITUIT]."

*Restitution coin struck by **Titus** in memory of **Claudius**.*

These restitution coins, explains Elvira Eliza Clain-Stefanelli of the Smithsonian Institution, "reveal a certain 'numismatic' interest which could have been responsible in part for initiating the issues, although undoubtedly the chief motivation was the attitude toward coins as an official chronicle of past glory."

Of course these restitution coins could hardly have been struck without some sort of collection of old coins to use as models.

The personification of Liberty, who appears on coins of the United States, is a direct, albeit distant, descendant of the Roman goddesses Roma and Libertas, both of whom appeared on coins issued nearly 2,000 years ago. The silver Peace dollar, considered by many to be the classic American coin, is in many ways a replica of the coins of ancient Rome. On the obverse, Peace is depicted in a bust, facing left, with a radiate crown. It is characteristic of radiate busts on Roman coins, and is intended to symbolize immortality. The reverse of the coin shows an eagle standing with its wings closed—another common motif on coins of ancient Greece and Rome. The obverse of the Mercury Head dime shows Liberty wearing a winged helmet—a design especially popular on the coins of the Roman Republic.

*United States silver dollar showing radiate bust of Peace, along
with a coin of the Roman Republic (c. 109 B.C.) showing similar
radiate bust of Sol. A coin of Ptolemy, King of Cyprus (c. first
century B.C.) shows the Roman Eagle.*

*Classic Mercury dime compared with an ancient coin of the Roman
Republic depicting a bust of Roma wearing the winged helmet.*

Of course we have many words relating to money and currency that have evolved from ancient words. One word for money matters, "pecuniary," comes from the Latin *pecus*, which means "ox." In ancient Babylonia the weight of one talent was the amount of gold needed to purchase one ox. And "shekel" was the Babylonian word for 1/100 of a talent. The abbreviation for the British penny was d. for hundreds of years, from the ancient Roman denarius, or silver penny. Even the all-American "dime" derives from the Old French word *disme*, which was evolved from the Latin word *decimus*, "one-tenth." In fact, when that denomination was first issued in the 1790s, it was actually called a "disme."

Money Myths Through the Ages

The numismatists who have studied some of the traditions associated with coins and money through the ages can also tell us some fascinating stories.

Everybody knows, for example, that coins are often considered to be "good luck" pieces. Many people have carried a "pocket piece," or lucky coin, around with them for years. I know a man who has carried the same silver dollar in his pocket daily for more than 25 years; another friend has carried an ancient Roman bronze sestertius (about the size of a silver dollar) for just about as long. I can't vouch for the ability of these amulets to bring luck, but I think my friends would have discarded them long ago if they didn't think they were somehow effective!

Have you ever pitched a penny into a pool, fountain, or wishing well? That tradition comes from an ancient Greek tradition of placing riches in sacred waters, or in the realm of a particular god, to obtain the god's protection.

The ancient Greeks also used to put a small silver coin, Charon's obol, into the mouth of a dead person. Its purpose was to serve as the fare paid to Charon, who had the job of ferrying the dead across the River Styx into the netherworld.

Another ancient custom was to put a coin in the cornerstone of a new building to ensure good luck and the durability of the structure itself.

Coins Tell a Story

A fascinating example of numismatic storytelling was described at the Eighth International Numismatic Conference in 1973, by the famous Israeli archaeologist and numismatist Dr. Ya'akov Meshorer.

He told of the excavations in 1964 of the ancient settlement of Ein-Gedi, on the shore of the Dead Sea. There was a house in that Jewish settlement that dated back to about the first century A.D. and had been preserved almost to its original height.

While the archaeologists were photographing this house, one of the workers accidentally knocked a piece of plaster off a high portion of the wall, and thus revealed an ancient clay oil lamp containing 139 small bronze coins (called perutahs or quadrantes), mostly issued by the procurators who ruled Judea under Rome between 6 and 66 A.D.

Meshorer concluded that these 139 coins could not have been a hoard in the usual sense, since their value was so small that one would not salt them away for the sake of saving or hiding money. At any rate, since the coins were hidden behind the plaster in the wall of the house, it was unlikely that the owner intended ever to recover the coins.

So, the archaeologist reconstructed the events leading up to the hiding of the money as follows:

"A Jew in the year 60 A.D. built his house, and while finishing it, before its last, plaster stage, decided to *hide* a *sacred* amount of money in the wall against the evil eye."

But why were there 139 coins? Was it chance, or was there a good reason behind this number? Meshorer has the answer. In ancient times the most sacred sum of money to the Jews was the half-shekel, since this was the amount each person paid as the annual tribute to the Temple. But, according to Meshorer, our first-century man did not want to simply put a single, silver half-shekel into his wall, since "the large number of coins apparently would make a better impression." The man also decided to put the money into a lamp—"a symbol of eternity."

But wait. Half a shekel was equal to only 128 of the small bronze coins. So why were there 139? Deduces the archaeologist: "One who came to the Temple to donate his tribute of half a shekel and gave it in different currency [than the usual silver currency of the city of Tyre, then officially used] to be changed by the money changers . . . had to add a sum equal to eight per cent of the tribute."

That fee was the same kind of fee banks charge today for changing one nation's currency to another's. And 8 percent of 139 is almost exactly 11, "thus putting in the lamp 139 quadrantes making the exact holy sum of half a shekel, in small change."

So, you can see some of the incredible detective work in which a numismatist can engage. And this fascinating example is only the beginning. Coins, as we will soon explore, can help tell us about many aspects of a civilization—our own or those of the past.

Anyone Can Collect

Coin collecting is the hobby of the rich no longer. Any child who finds an old penny in the dirt can understand the fascination of collecting coins.

Many adults over the years have become avid collectors of United States coins because their jobs involved handling a lot of small change, and they began to put aside sets of coins of various dates and mints. Then at the end of each day they would buy them from their employer at face value. Bank tellers, grocery clerks, vending-machine servicemen or operators, and many others have had the opportunity over the years to develop huge and complete collections of United States coins, never paying more than face value for any of them.

Alas, those were the good old days of coin collecting in the United States. Today a youngster can build only a limited collection by taking coins from circulation. Most of the cents now circulating in the United States are of the "Lincoln Memorial" variety. The old "wheat back" cents have almost disappeared from circulation just as the Indian Head cents slowly vanished from circulation earlier this century.

And of course the United States silver coinage—dimes, quarters, half-dollars, and dollars—was discontinued as circulating coins in 1964, and replaced by the nickel-clad coins you can now find in your pockets. The silver coins have long been pulled out of circulation because the value of the silver in them far exceeded the nominal value of the coins. Nevertheless, you may find some older relative or friend has put away a small cache of the old silver coins and perhaps will let you go through the jarful, boxful, or bagful and buy for face value those coins you need to fill gaps in your collection.

Treasure Hunters

Many thousands of Americans have bought treasure-hunting devices—actually simple metal detectors—and have combed parks and beach areas for old coins. You'll come up with a tin can or a piece of scrap iron many more times than you will find a coin. Nevertheless, you'll have fun in the hunt. Beware, however, since many local, state, and National Park areas are off limits to treasure hunters of this sort, and strict penalties and fines can result.

Today there are some five to ten million coin collectors in the United States. They come from all walks of life and all backgrounds. Some are most interested in collecting coins of our own nation. Others specialize in different fields, such as the coins of the country from which their parents or grandparents came, or the coins of a country that they once visited and of which they are particularly fond. Still others collect paper money, tokens, medals, military decorations, misstruck coins or errors, ancient coins, foreign crown-sized coins, Byzantine coins, coins of Bible Days, and many more.

There are entire libraries of books on all of these various areas of coin collecting. This book will introduce you to the more popular areas of coin collecting today. Perhaps one of those areas will especially interest you, and you will go on to other references, which can offer you more detailed and specific information. Or you may become one of the many generalists in the field of coin collecting, trying to assemble a collection with one or two examples from many different areas of numismatics.

Whichever you choose, we are sure that you will enjoy this hobby. Through it you will make many new friends and learn a great deal about many things. As a side benefit you may also make an excellent investment. We'll talk about that briefly later in the book, but if your love is mainly *making* money and not *learning* about it, this book is not for you.

Don't be in too big a hurry. Learn as you collect. Buy carefully and evaluate the marketplace as you continue to buy. Don't let your desire to have "the best" or "the biggest" collection make you into a careless collector, or into one who simply accumulates coins. If you concentrate only on filling your book with all of the dates and all of the mint marks you will be cheating yourself out of one of the best parts of the hobby—the story behind the coin. One always exists.

Listen carefully to the advice of my friend Edward Janis, a past president of the New York Numismatic Club, who likes to tell young and eager coin collectors that they really can never be the *owners* of the coins in their collection.

"You are just the temporary *custodian* of the coins," Janis explains. "In many cases the coins were around long before you were, and there is every good chance they will be around long after you are gone."

So enjoy your coins. Study them. Learn from them.

The coin of the realm—whether the United States today or ancient Greece of more than 2,000 years ago—can also be a key to the mind. The doors this key can open will be limited only by your imagination.

2. What Are Coins?

World Without Money

Can you imagine a world without money? How would we buy, sell, tip, flip? Hard to visualize, isn't it?

Yet that's just the way it was at the beginning.

Each family or tribe was a self-sufficient unit. People in those days had no fancy homes or cars to worry about. Their main preoccupations were staying alive and having children. The members of each family or group were responsible for their own clan—for hunting food, finding shelter, and obtaining suitable clothing.

But as man and his societies developed, so too did his need to deal in some way with other men. That was the day, perhaps, that one fellow—an especially good hunter—found that he had more meat, or fish, or skins, than he needed. And he went to another person and said, "What will you give me if I give you some of this meat?"

Perhaps the second party to this deal was an especially skilled craftsman. Maybe he even made the kinds of weapons that our hunter friend used to kill animals. "I will give you two sharp throwing stones for that meat," he might have said.

That must have been roughly how it began: the first deal. Soon people were haggling over swaps of all kinds. This practice of exchanging goods for goods became known as barter. It sometimes still occurs today.

In ancient times, as man became more civilized, barter became an increasingly difficult way to trade. Imagine the poor fellow who had just caught a dozen fine fish and wanted to trade them for something he needed. He might have to wander for hours—or days—before finding someone who both wanted his fish *and* had that special something he would accept in return for them. If he had to spend too much time searching out a trade, his fresh fish would spoil, and wouldn't be much good to anyone.

Because of this kind of impracticality, barter as a way of exchange gradually died out. To replace it man needed something that could be used instead of all these tradeable goods—something that people could use to swap for what they needed. Whatever this "thing" was to be, it had to be universally acceptable—at least within a tribe or region—as well as available, durable (unlike the fish), and easily divided. That commodity developed differently in the various primitive civilizations. Sometimes it was beads, shells, grain, or stones. Whatever it was, it was the earliest form of money.

The Earliest Money

Many people believe that one of the earliest forms of money was the cowrie shells which are common on the islands in the Pacific Ocean. These could be strung together and worn as ornaments, and as such became a sign of wealth. Before long, as the story goes, everybody was trading their extra goods for cowrie shells and making the shells into all kinds of bracelets, necklaces, and other ornaments.

It worked like this: A hunter had a good day and killed several animals. He knew that his family could use only a certain amount of this meat before it spoiled, so he traded the remainder to someone for several strands of shells. Later, when he needed new hunting equipment, clothes, or even some more food, he would trade some or all of his shells to another person in exchange for what he or his family needed.

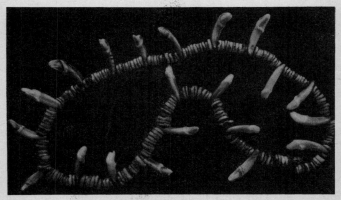

Necklace of shells and canine teeth used by natives of the Solomon Islands.

Siberian Brick Tea, used as a trading commodity since ancient times, was in use as late as the twentieth century.

Thus the trading process was becoming streamlined from the previous cumbersome method of trading goods for goods. A few of the different kinds of commodities that were once used as money were livestock, pelts, cocoanuts, beads, tools, fishhooks, animal teeth, bricks made of tea, and bars of salt.

People living on Yap Island in the Pacific used round stones with holes in the middle of them as money. These stones, called *fei*, ranged in size up to 10 feet in diameter. The people of Yap would lean these giant stones against trees in front of their homes to show how wealthy they were.

As the "money" method of trading caught on, problems arose. One obvious problem was the matter of conversion from one primitive "currency" to another. Today there are mathematical formulas for converting United States dollars into Italian lira or

Fei, *or stone money, of the Yap Islands.*

British pounds sterling, for example. But in ancient days it wasn't always easy to convert values from cocoanuts to whale teeth. One factor, of course, was that there was no standardization, since different items had different values to different people.

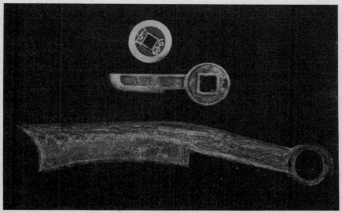

Spade money of ancient China.

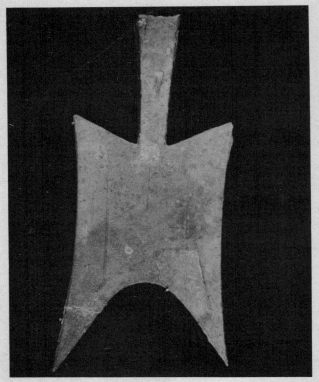

Ancient Chinese knife money, key money, and modern cash coin.

In ancient China the people used to use spades, chisels, knives, and pieces of cloth as money. But these items weren't too easy to carry around in quantity. This led the Chinese, about 700 B.C.—interestingly, about the same time the first Western coinage was issued—to create their own actual money. The rulers ordered small bronze copies of the tools and cloth shirts to be made, and these facsimiles were used in trade instead of the articles themselves. Today some collectors are lucky enough to own an example of Chinese shirt money, knife money, spade money, or razor money. By about 255 B.C. this kind of money disappeared, and its place was taken by the round "cash" coins, with square holes in the center of each coin. Very similar coins were made in China for the next 2,000 or so years, and remain in use in some parts of China to this very day. And, happily, examples of this interesting "cash" coinage can be obtained from many coin dealers for less than a dollar!

First Western Coins

The honor of issuing the first Western coinage probably goes to the country of Lydia in Asia Minor, with Aegina, another Greek state, apparently a close second. In Lydia the first "coins" were struck about 640 B.C. They were lumps of electrum—a natural alloy of gold and silver—stamped with a design on one side only. Some of the earliest designs were goats, cocks, foxes, and lions. The other side of these earliest coins showed only a striated surface resulting from marks scratched onto the top of the anvil on which the coins were struck. Soon another coin of Lydia was struck with the head of a lion on one side and three irregular punch marks from the anvil on the other side. Unfortunately the composition of the electrum from which these coins were struck varied greatly, and they therefore left something to be desired as a regular commodity of trade.

Before actual coinage developed, lumps of metal, ingots, and wedges were used as money for some time. In fact, the word "coin" is derived from the Latin word *cuneus*, which means "wedge." However, the use of these wedges or ingots was difficult, since they had to be accurately weighed at the time of each transaction. Eventually merchants got the idea of putting their marks on some of these lumps so they could be recognized in case one of them came back. Thus a merchant would not need to reweigh each piece of metal again, speeding up the transaction. (One problem of this technique, however, was that the ingots were of irregular shapes, and it wasn't too difficult for a dishonest trader to nip off an odd edge here or there, thus cheating on the actual original marked weight of the piece. This is a ploy that we will encounter later, even as more sophisticated coinage develops.)

The Egyptian king Croesus of Lydia, who ruled from 560 to 546 B.C., ordered his own official marks to be placed on lumps of gold

Coin of King Croesus of Lydia, showing on the obverse the head of a lion facing the head of a bull.

and silver—the first time a government sanctioned coins and guaranteed their purity and weights.

The designs on those coins were the heads of a lion and a bull facing each other on one side, and punch marks from the anvil on the other. A short time later, when Aegina issued silver coins stamped on one side with a smooth-shelled sea turtle, the ruler of this state, too, was making the same guarantee. As the practice of issuing coinage spread to the city-states of ancient Greece, each of them developed its own characteristic symbols, or mint marks—a practice that we have continued to this day in the United States.

Although the first coins were gold, silver, and bronze, other metals, such as lead, iron, tin, copper, zinc, and other combinations, have been used as coins at various times. In early days silver and gold were popular because they could easily be converted into decorative articles. Bronze at once became popular when it was introduced because it could readily be made into agricultural tools or weapons. Eventually the main criteria for using a particular metal for coinage were the metal's value as a medium of exchange, the ease of making the metal into a coin, and the ability of the metal to withstand continuous wear and tear once it was made into a coin.

Eventually paper money developed as a "note" to promise that the actual commodity of value was stored away in a safe place to back it up. Paper money existed almost 1,000 years ago in China, and it was used about 900 years ago in Europe. Soon the merchants who often dealt in exchanging money found they could make a good living by exchanging the money of one country for that of another. In Italy and then in England, these merchants, who were to become the first bankers, found that they could issue paper receipts for money they had stored away safely—today we would say they had the money "on deposit."

This system worked as long as the public had confidence in the bankers. And as the people gained more confidence, the practice of issuing these banknotes became even more widespread. Eventually the governments moved in to protect both the bankers and their depositors, and finally the governments themselves began to issue currencies and to guarantee their uniform values.

How Coins Are Made

It is interesting that methods for making coins are almost exactly the same today as they were more than 2,000 years ago, except that modern machines produce coins automatically and rapidly.

The United States mint at Philadelphia is equipped to produce eight million coins in each eight-hour shift. The facility operates two shifts a day and thus produces four billion coins per year. Those operations that are now automated and computerized were done laboriously by hand in ancient times.

The four basic steps to making coins are:

1. Preparing the metal
2. Preparing the blanks upon which the coins will be struck
3. Engraving and preparing the dies
4. Striking the coins

The metal for striking coins was prepared in even ancient times by mixing together two or more different kinds of metals. The pure metals—gold, silver, or copper—were never used alone since they were too soft. Thus the metals were melted and mixed to the proper alloy.

Once this was accomplished the blanks, also called flans, were cast in molds. The molds varied according to the types of coins that were being made. In ancient Israel at about the time of Jesus, for example, the blanks were cast by pouring the molten bronze into trays that had dozens of round, shallow sockets drilled into them. Each of these sockets was connected to the next, so the liquid metal filled each of them. Sometimes there was both a top and bottom to the flan molds, and this made for even more uniform flans. After the metal in these molds had cooled, the strips of flans were removed.

An assistant to the minter would reheat each strip and then place the first blank of the strip in between two striking dies on a sturdy base. The bottom die may well have been secured in a heavy tree trunk. The man who was to strike the coins then hit the top die with a hammer, thus striking the design into the coin. The assistant then pulled the strip one blank further along, and the process was repeated.

In ancient Greece and Rome, the gold, silver, and some of the bronze coins were apparently struck one at a time, having first been cast in molds as button-shaped blanks, then prepared individually for striking. Striking coins in strips was apparently popular among many of the nations of the Middle East.

The process of pulling strips of coins through the dies and striking them was obviously carried out quite quickly, and the resultant coins were struck off center frequently. Indeed, ancient coins are struck imperfectly more often than not; it is a rare ancient coin that is both firmly struck and perfectly centered on both sides. Once the strips of blanks were struck, they were chopped apart

Silver denarius of the Roman Republic, c. 48 B.C., *showing the goddess Moneta on the obverse, and the minter's tools on the reverse.*

into coins and the remaining metal scraps were melted down once again. Many of these small bronze coins of ancient Israel still show clearly how they were chopped away from the strips.

Most ancient coins were apparently struck from blanks that had been heated just before striking. The metal was softer after heating, and because of this the dies lasted longer. Coins could be struck on cold blanks, but the wear and tear on the dies would cause them to break and become deformed rapidly. If they are to last at all, of course, the dies for striking coins must always be made from a metal that is harder than the metal of the coin itself. Thus bronze dies would suffice for striking gold coins, but iron or steel would have to be used to successfully strike large numbers of bronze and silver coins.

Two dies are necessary to strike each coin—one for the obverse design and one for the reverse design.

The first coins, as mentioned earlier, were struck with an obverse die only, the reverse of the coin receiving an incuse impression from the anvil on which it was struck.

In ancient days dies were engraved by hand. It must have been a difficult task. First, the engravings were so intricate and tiny. Second, the engraver had to work completely backward—the shallowest points on the die became the deepest points on the coin, and vice versa. Finally, the dies had to be a mirror image of how the coins would eventually look, since the striking process reverses the design. (Interestingly, some beginning diecutters in ancient times apparently had a difficult time understanding this principle, and instead of engraving the mirror image of the inscription they desired, they inscribed the true image into the die. Thus when the coins were struck they carried the inscription in mirror image, known to numismatists as "retrograde.")

It is worth noting that the Chinese did not adopt any of the techniques for striking coins until the twentieth century. Before that time they cast their coins just as the early Greeks cast their round blanks.

Only rarely in ancient **Greece and** Rome were coins cast in molds which already had the designs engraved in them. This practice was, however, usually used in making the large bronze coins of the early Roman Republican period. But the vast majority of ancient coins—indeed of all coins—have been struck and not cast. When we later get into the discussion of fakes and forgeries, this factor will be especially important, so keep it in mind.

3. United States Coins

You can start collecting coins right now. Just put your hand into your pocket. What have you got? Cent, nickel, dime? Check the dates and the mint marks and put the coins in a special place. Now you have the beginnings of a coin collection. Watch how quickly it can grow. And you'll be surprised how much you can learn in a relatively short time. You'll learn about minting techniques and the various series of U.S. coins, and of course you'll learn a lot about the history of your country.

The first American money was probably the belts of Indian beads called wampum. Even though the king of England outlawed wampum as a currency in 1661, it continued to be used here as a medium of exchange along with tobacco, pelts, gunpowder, and rifle shot. Indeed, in 1634 the Massachusetts court held that musket bullets of full size should pass as currency equal to 1 farthing each—a farthing was equal to a quarter-penny—but no one was compelled to take more than 12 pence worth of the musket balls at one time. Later Dutch, French, and English settlers used money from their own lands as well as the Spanish American coins that circulated widely in those days.

On May 27, 1652, the first American Colonial mint was established in Boston, without the king's approval. Silver coins were struck at the Boston mint until it was closed in about 1683 upon the death of mintmaster John Hull. This is where the famous New England shillings were struck. These were simply discs of silver with "N.E." (for New England) on one side and "XII" on the

Pine Tree Shilling

other. "XII" is the Roman numeral 12, which stood for the coin's denomination of 12 pence or 1 shilling.

These simple coins were very easily counterfeited, so new motifs—the famous "tree money"—were designed. These silver coins were struck in denominations of shilling, sixpence, and threepence, showing either oak, pine, or willow trees on each type. Most of these coins carry the date 1652.

Coins were also issued by individual states in the seventeenth and eighteenth centuries, and soon the young federal government began to experiment with coinage of its own.

Fugio Cent

On July 6, 1786, the United States Congress issued a resolution authorizing "the contractor for the copper coinage to stamp on one side of each piece the following device, viz: thirteen circles linked together, a small circle in the middle, with the words 'United States' round it; and in the centre, the words 'We are one'; on the other side of the same piece the following device, viz: a dial with the hours expressed on the face of it; a meridian sun above on one side of which is the word 'Fugio.' "

The word "Fugio" was taken to mean "time flies," and the inscription "Mind Your Business" was added to the obverse of the coin's design. It was said that the design of the Fugio cent was suggested by Benjamin Franklin, hence it has also been referred to as the Franklin cent. The Fugio cent was first struck in New York City, and later in New Haven, Conn., and Rupert, Vt., among other places.

The Congress passed a resolution establishing the United States mint on December 6, 1790. It was signed by President Washington on March 3, 1791. Another piece of legislation supporting the idea of a national mint was passed on April 2, 1792. It was that same year that the first United States mint was established in Philadelphia, then the U.S. capital, under the directorship of David Rittenhouse. The mint was the first public building erected by the United States government for a public purpose.

It was also in 1792 that Congress established a system of coinage based on the decimal system, in contrast with the British system of pounds, shillings, and pence.

That first mint in Philadelphia was nothing like any of the mints in our nation today. The first ledger of the U.S. mint contains such items as "Straw, hay and horse medicine—$2.00; Watch dog—$3.00; Yard alarm bell—$17.82; Director's salary—$2,000.00; 6 lbs. old copper—$1.00."

In 1816 the first U.S. mint at Philadelphia burned and was mostly destroyed. A new and better mint was designed and built, being completed in 1833.

From those first minting establishments of our nation, United States mints have issued many fascinating series of coins—right up to the popular bicentennial issues of 1976.

United States Mint Marks

You may be familiar with only two United States mint marks, D for the Denver mint and S for the San Francisco mint. However, there have been several other official United States mints. Here is a list of them, with the dates they operated and the mint marks they used.

Mint	Dates	Mint mark
Philadelphia, Pa.	1792 to date	None*
Dahlonega, Ga.	1838–1861 (struck gold coins only)	D
Charlotte, N.C.	1838–1861 (struck gold coins only)	C
New Orleans, La.	1838–1861; 1879–1909	O
San Francisco, Cal.	1854–1955; 1968 to date	S
Carson City, Nev.	1870–1893	CC
Denver, Colo.	1906 to date	D

*Except between 1942 and 1945, when the mint in Philadelphia issued the part-silver war nickels, and on these coins the mintmark P appeared above the building on the reverse

In 1965, when the Denver and Philadelphia mints—the only two then operating— began to issue the copper-clad coins, the use of mint marks was discontinued. The mint marks were returned to use and their former glory in 1968, incidentally the same year the new U.S. mint in San Francisco again began to produce coins.

Where to Find Mint Marks

Here is a list to help you find the mint marks on United States coins.

Coin	Location and Mint Marks
Half Cents	No mint marks
Large Cents	No mint marks
Flying Eagle Cents	No mint marks
Indian Head Cents	Mint marks on 1908 and 1909 only, S, reverse bottom beneath wreath
Two Cent Piece	No mint marks
Three Cent Piece	Mint mark O on 1851 only, on reverse to right of III
Five Cents (Shield)	No mint marks
Liberty Head Nickel	Mint marks S and D on 1912 only, on reverse to left of "cents"
Buffalo Nickel	Mint marks S and D on reverse beneath "FIVE CENTS"
Jefferson Nickel	Mint marks P, D, and S 1942 to 1945 on reverse above building dome; until 1968, D and S on reverse to right of building; 1968 onward, on obverse, lower right below date
Half Dime	No mint marks
Liberty Seated Half Dimes	Mint marks O and S on reverse beneath or within wreath
One Dime	No mint mark
Liberty Seated Dime	Mint marks O, S, and CC on reverse beneath or within wreath
Mercury Head Dime	Mint marks D and S on reverse to left below fasces
Roosevelt Dime	Mint marks D and S until 1964 on reverse bottom-left of torch; after 1968 on obverse above date

Coin	Location and Mint Marks
Twenty Cent Piece	Mint marks S and CC on reverse beneath eagle
Quarter Dollar	No mint marks
Liberty Seated Quarter	Mint marks O, S, and CC on reverse beneath eagle
Liberty Head Quarter	Mint marks O, S, and D on reverse beneath eagle
Standing Liberty Quarter	Mint marks D and S on obverse, above-left of date
Washington Quarter	Mint marks D and S until 1964 on reverse beneath eagle; after 1968 on obverse in back of neck
Half Dollar	Mint mark O on 1838–1839, on obverse between drape folds and date
Liberty Seated Half	Mint marks S, O, and CC on reverse beneath eagle
Liberty Head Half	Mint marks O, S, and D on reverse beneath eagle
Walking Liberty Half	Mint marks D and S on reverse to left of "HALF DOLLAR"
Franklin Half	Mint marks D and S on reverse above Liberty Bell
Kennedy Half	Mint mark D until 1964 on reverse near eagle claw with wreath; after 1968 (added S on proof coins only) on obverse below neck
One Dollar	No mint marks
Liberty Seated Dollar	Mint marks S and CC on reverse beneath eagle
Liberty Head (Morgan) Dollar	Mint marks O, D, S, and CC on reverse beneath eagle
Liberty Head (Peace) Dollar	Mint marks D and S on reverse below-left of eagle's wing
Eisenhower Dollar	Mint marks D and S on obverse, above date

Coin	Location and Mint Marks
Gold Dollar	Mint marks C, D, O, and S on reverse beneath wreath
Liberty Cap Quarter Eagle	No mint marks
Classic Head Quarter Eagle	Mint marks C, D, and O on obverse above date
Coronet Quarter Eagle	Mint marks C, D, O, and S on reverse beneath eagle
Indian Head Quarter Eagle	Mint mark D on reverse to left of eagle claw
Three Dollar Gold	Mint marks S, D, and O on reverse beneath wreath
Liberty Cap Half Eagle	No mint marks
Classic Head Half Eagle	Mint marks C and D on obverse above date
Coronet Half Eagle	Mint marks CC, O, D, S, and C on reverse beneath eagle
Indian Head Half Eagle	Mint marks D, O, and S on reverse to left of eagle claw
Liberty Cap Eagle	No mint marks
Coronet Eagle	Mint marks S, CC, O, and D on reverse beneath eagle
Indian Head Eagle	Mint marks D and S on reverse to left of eagle claw
Coronet Double Eagle	Mint marks O, S, CC, and D on reverse beneath eagle
Standing Liberty Double Eagle	Mint marks D and S on obverse above date

Collecting U.S. Coins

Collectors often decide to try to obtain one of each type of coin issued by the United States, and this is called "type collecting." Others choose to complete a set of dates and mint marks of a particular series, such as cents, or even just Indian Head cents, and this is called "series collecting." As in all other fields of coin collecting, the beginner is best off establishing a general collection to learn as much as possible about the coins of the United States. Later a specialty may develop, and as one particular series is completed, the collector may go on to something else.

Here is a general survey of the types of coins issued by the United States, and when they were issued.

Coin	Dates
Half Cents (copper)	

Liberty Cap   1793–1797

Draped Bust   1800–1808

Turban Head   1809–1836

Braided Hair   1840–1857

Coin	Dates

Cents
Large Cents (copper)

Chain   1793

Wreath   1793

Liberty Cap   1793–1796

Draped Bust   1796–1807

Coin	*Dates*

Turban Head   1808–1814

Coronet   1816–1839

Braided Hair   1839–1857

Small Cents (copper-nickel 1856–1864; bronze 1864–1942, and
1946 to date; steel 1943; copper 1944–1945)

Flying Eagle   1856–1858

Coin	*Dates*

Indian Head | 1859–1909

Lincoln Head—wheat rev. | 1909–1959
Lincoln Head—memorial rev. | 1959 to date

Two Cents (bronze) | 1864–1873

Three Cents (nickel) | 1865–1889

Three Cents (silver) | 1851–1873

Coin	Dates

Five Cents (nickel)

Shield   1866–1883

Liberty Head   1883–1912

Buffalo (or Indian Head) 1913–1938

Jefferson   1938 to date

Half Dimes (silver)

Bust (or Liberty Head)   1794–1837

Coin	*Dates*

Liberty Seated   1837–1873

Dimes (silver)

Bust   1796–1837

Liberty Seated   1837–1891

Liberty Head (Barber)   1892–1916

Winged Head Liberty   1916–1945
(or Mercury Head)

Coin	*Dates*
 Roosevelt	 1946 to date
 Twenty Cent Piece (silver)	 1875–1878

Quarters (silver until 1964, clad copper thereafter)

 Bust	 1796–1838
 Liberty Seated	 1838–1891

Coin	Dates

Liberty Head (Barber)　　　　1892–1916

Liberty Standing　　　　1916–1930

Washington (silver)　　　1932–1964
Washington (clad)　　　　1965–1974

Washington-Bicentennial　　1976 (issued 1975)
(clad and silver issues)

Coin	Dates

Half Dollars (silver until 1964, clad thereafter with exceptions)

Bust   1794–1839

Liberty Seated   1839–1891

Liberty Head (Barber)   1892–1915

Coin	*Dates*

| Liberty Walking | 1916–1947 |

Franklin	1948–1963
Kennedy (silver)	1964
Kennedy (silver-clad)	1965–1970
Kennedy (clad)	1971–1974

| Kennedy-Bicentennial (clad and silver issues) | 1976 (issued 1975) |

Coin	Dates

Dollars (silver until 1935, clad nickel thereafter with exceptions)

Bust   1794–1839

Liberty Seated   1840–1873

Liberty Head (Morgan)   1878–1921

Coin	*Dates*

Peace   1921–1935

Eisenhower (silver-clad)   1971–1972
Eisenhower (nickel-clad)   1971–1974

Eisenhower-Bicentennial   1976 (issued 1975)
(silver and nickel-clad issues)

Coin	Dates

Trade Dollars (silver)   1873–1878
Proofs only   1879–1885
Gold Dollars

Liberty Head   1849–1854

Indian Headdress   1854–1889
Quarter Eagles ($2.50 gold)

Liberty Cap   1796–1807

Liberty Head   1808–1834

Coin	Dates
Ribbon	1834–1839
Coronet	1840–1907
Indian Head Incuse	1908–1929
Three Dollar (gold)	1854–1889
Four Dollar (gold) Patterns Proofs only	1854–1889 1879–1880

Coin	*Dates*

Half Eagles ($5 gold)

Liberty Cap   1795–1807

Liberty Head   1807–1812

Ribbon   1834–1838

Coronet   1839–1908

Coin	*Dates*

Indian Head Incuse   1908–1929

Eagles ($10 gold)

Liberty Cap   1795–1804

Coronet   1838–1907

Indian Head   1907–1933

Coin	*Dates*

Double Eagles ($20 gold)

Coronet   1849–1907

Liberty Standing (Saint-Gaudens)   1907–1933

U.S. Commemoratives

The United States has also issued an interesting series of silver and gold commemorative coins. These coins were never meant to go into general circulation, and were struck only to honor special occasions such as expositions and states' anniversaries, or other historical events related to the founding of the United States. There are fifty different types of silver commemorative coins issued by the United States until now, the vast majority of them being half-dollars. There have been ten United States gold commemorative coins. Here is a list of all of them.

Mint Mark	Date	Type

| None | 1892–1893 | Columbian Exposition Half Dollar |
| None | 1893 | Isabella Quarter Dollar |

Mint Mark	Date	Type

Mint Mark	Date	Type
None	1900	Lafayette Dollar
S	1915	Panama Pacific Exposition Half Dollar
None	1918	Illinois Centennial Half Dollar
None	1920	Maine Centennial Half Dollar
None	1920–1921	Pilgrim Tercentenary Half Dollar
None	1921	Alabama Centennial Half Dollar

None	1921	Missouri Centennial Half Dollar

None	1922	Grant Memorial Half Dollar

Mint Mark	Date	Type
S	1923	Monroe Doctrine Centennial Half Dollar
None	1923	Huguenot-Walloon Tercentenary Half Dollar
None	1925	Lexington-Concord Sesquicentennial Half Dollar
None	1925	Stone Mountain Memorial Half Dollar
S	1925	California Diamond Jubilee Half Dollar

Mint Mark	Date	Type
None	1925	Fort Vancouver Centennial Half Dollar
None	1926	Sesquicentennial–American Independence Half Dollar
D, S	1926, 1928, 1933, 1934, 1936, 1937, 1938, 1939	Oregon Trail Memorial Half Dollar
None	1927	Vermont Sesquicentennial Half Dollar

Mint Mark	Date	Type
None	1928	Hawaiian Sesquicentennial Half Dollar

Mint Mark	Date	Type
D, S	1934–1938	Texas Centennial Half Dollar
None	1934	Maryland Tercentenary Half Dollar
D, S	1934–1938	Daniel Boone Bicentennial Half Dollar
None	1935	Connecticut Tercentenary Half Dollar

None	1935	Hudson, N.Y. Half Dollar

None	1935	Old Spanish Trail Half Dollar
D, S	1935–1936	California Pacific Exposition Half Dollar
D, S	1936	Providence, R.I., Tercentenary Half Dollar
D, S	1936	Columbia, S.C., Sesquicentennial Half Dollar
D, S	1936	Cincinnati Musical Center Half Dollar
D, S	1935–1939	Arkansas Centennial Half Dollar
None	1936	Robinson, Ark., Centennial Half Dollar

Mint Mark	Date	Type
None	1936	Long Island Tercentenary Half Dollar
None	1936	Cleveland Great Lakes Exposition Half Dollar
None	1936	Wisconsin Territorial Centennial Half Dollar
None	1936	Bridgeport, Conn., Centennial Half Dollar
None	1936	Lynchburg, Va., Sesquicentennial Half Dollar
None	1936	Elgin, Ill., Centennial Half Dollar
None	1936	Albany, N.Y., Charter Half Dollar
S	1936	San Francisco–Oakland Bay Bridge Half Dollar
None	1936	York County, Me., Tercentenary Half Dollar
None	1936	Delaware Tercentenary Half Dollar
None	1936	Battle of Gettysburg Half Dollar
None	1936	Norfolk, Va., Bicentennial Half Dollar
None	1937	Roanoke Island, N.C., Half Dollar
None	1937	Battle of Antietam Half Dollar
None	1938	New Rochelle, N.Y., Half Dollar
None	1946	Iowa Statehood Centennial Half Dollar
D, S	1946–1951	Booker T. Washington Memorial Half Dollar
D, S	1951–1954	Washington-Carver Commemorative Half Dollar

GOLD COMMEMORATIVE COINS OF THE U.S.

| None | 1903 (Jefferson and McKinley) | Louisiana Purchase Exposition Dollar |

Mint Mark	Date	Type
None	1904–1905	Lewis and Clark Exposition Dollar
S	1915	Panama Pacific Exposition Dollar
S	1915	Panama Pacific Quarter Eagle
S	1915	Panama Pacific $50 Round
S	1915	Panama Pacific $50 Octagonal
None	1916–1917	McKinley Memorial Dollar
None	1922	Grant Memorial Dollar
None	1926	Philadelphia Sesquicentennial Quarter Eagle

United States Proof Coins

Many collectors of United States coins have chosen to save only proof coins or proof sets. Proofs are coins struck by the mint especially for collectors. They are struck from special dies, which have been highly polished until they have a mirrorlike finish. Special blanks are also carefully treated before being struck. The resulting coins have special proof surfaces. Since the proof coins are struck as collectors' items, it could be argued that strictly speaking they are not coins at all, but really medals.

Equipment for the first Brilliant Proof coins was installed at the Philadelphia mint in 1817. From that time until the early 1850s, proof coins were struck mainly as presentation pieces to dignitaries. They were apparently available to collectors on special request, but there were few collectors to request them in those days. By 1858 the proof sets were generally made available to collectors, and this practice continued until 1916, when the production of proof coins was temporarily halted. Proof coinage was not resumed until 1936, and they were made until 1942. World War II again caused a halt in proof production, but it was resumed between 1950 and 1964. A critical nationwide coin shortage occurred in 1965, and the mints had to use all of their resources to produce coins for circulation. When proof production was resumed in 1968, they were issued by the San Francisco mint.

Each person can order as many as five United States Proof Sets each year. Orders are filled by the mint on a first-come, first-served basis, so the wise collector submits his payment as soon as possible after he receives the mint's order blank. If you would like to obtain United States Proof Sets, you can be put on the regular mailing list for order blanks and other information by writing to: The Bureau of the Mint, 55 Mint Street, San Francisco, CA 94175.

4. World Coins

You can buy rather complete catalogues of modern world coins. One of the latest is the *Standard Catalog of World Coins* by Krause and Michler. It covers nearly three hundred countries with tens of thousands of coins listed by country and date from the mid-1800s to the present. It's bigger than the telephone book of most cities!

Because of the huge numbers of coins issued worldwide in the last few hundred years, you will not find in this chapter anything like a listing of the foreign coins that are available to collectors. Instead I will just offer a few tips on collecting world coins, and a list that will help you identify many coins of the world.

Collecting foreign coins is a wonderful way to begin. Foreign coins can be inexpensive, yet are rich with the world's history. It

isn't hard to begin collecting foreign coins. If you check the advertisements in the weekly or monthly coin publications you will find
that you can buy the more recent foreign "minors" by the pound
for a very reasonable price per coin. This type of collecting can be
very rewarding if you set a goal for yourself—for example, one
coin from each nation of the world. In so doing you'll have to keep
up on foreign affairs, since there have been many changes in the
world community in the past 25 years.

You can also get foreign coins at face value from the currency-
exchange merchants, who will charge a nominal percentage for
their services. These merchants can be found in most large cities in
the United States.

Some collectors of foreign coins specialize in collecting gold
coins of the world, others specialize in the "crowns."

The first coin that fit today's description of a "crown" was the
five-shilling coin issued under King Edward VI in 1551. It is interesting that the name "crown" was given to the coin not because it
was issued by the king, but because it was struck of high-quality
silver. Many nations have issued crown-sized coins in this century
(the crowns of the world include the silver-dollar-sized coins).

The first "crown" struck under King Edward VI in 1551.

While the minor coins of most nations are usually inexpensive,
the crown-sized pieces often command a premium, especially in
the higher grades. They are also thought to be a better long-term
investment, as are the gold coins of the world, especially those
with numismatic value in addition to the metal value.

Since Canada and Mexico are the immediate neighbors of the
United States, the coins of both nations are popular here. Canada

is a Commonwealth nation and its coins invariably bear the portrait of the ruling monarch of Great Britain. The Canadian mint does not issue proof coins, but prooflike or uncirculated sets are available from: The Royal Canadian Mint, Coins Uncirculated, P.O. Box 470, Ottawa 2, Ontario, Canada.

From the "pieces of eight" to the pesos and centavos of today, the coins of Mexico also have quite a following in the United States. The Spanish milled dollar of eight reals was often known as the piece of eight. The coin was minted at Mexico City from 1732 to 1821, and was often cut into eight segments or "bits" to use as small change. The "two-bit" piece was the ancestor of our 25-cent piece, or quarter.

The coins of Great Britain are also popular among American collectors, since we have so much of a common heritage with the English, including our language. Coins have been issued in Great Britain since ancient times, and there are literally dozens of interesting series one could begin to collect. The old British monetary system was based on the pound, which contained 12 shillings and 240 pence. Pence were abbreviated with the letter "d," a holdover from the designation for the Roman denarius. Beginning in 1968, England changed to a new monetary system based on the pound being broken into 100 new pence.

Many collectors like to begin their foreign-coin collections with a few coins from a country or area they have visited. Others like to collect coins from the nation of their heritage. Thus in the United States there are many collectors of Irish, German, Scandinavian, Eastern European, Spanish, Dutch, and Russian coins, as well as others. Over the past decade there has been increasing interest in coins of Japan and China. And there is no doubt with the increased awareness of black Americans of their heritage, the coins of many African nations will also become quite popular.

Identifying Foreign Coins

Sometimes foreign coins are very difficult to identify even though they are inscribed in the Latin alphabet. Those coins inscribed in the Greek or Cyrillic alphabets are sometimes even more difficult to identify, as are those in Hebrew and some of the other alphabets. To identify those coins it will be necessary for you to seek help in a volume specializing in the particular coins or areas. However, here is a list of some of the key words that will help you identify many foreign coins with legends in the Latin alphabet.

AFRICA PORTUGUEZA	Angola
AFRIQUE DE L'OUEST	West African States
AFRIQUE EQUATORIALE FRANÇAISE	French Equatorial Africa
AFRIQUE ORIENTALE	Mozambique
ALGERIE	Algeria
AMERICA CENTRAL	Costa Rica
ANGL	Great Britain
ANTILLEN	Netherland Antilles
APOSTOLORVM PRINCEPS	Papal States
AUSTRIAE	Austria
BANK DEUTSCHER LANDER	Germany (West)
BELGIQUE	Belgium
BOLIVIANA	Bolivia
BORNEO	British North Borneo
BRASIL	Brazil
BRASILLIAE	Brazil
BRITANNIE	Brittany
BRITT	Great Britain
BUNDESREPUBLIK DEUTSCHLAND	Federal Republic of Germany
CAMBODGE	Cambodia

CAMEROUN	Cameroon
CAYENNE	French Guiana
CCCP	USSR
CENTRAFRICAINE	Central African Republic
CESKOSLOVENSKA	Czechoslovakia
CHERIFIEN	Morocco
DANMARK	Denmark
DANSK AMERIKANSK	Danish West Indies
DEUTSCHE DEMOKRATISCHE REPUBLIK	German Democratic Republic
DEUTSCHES REICH	Germany
DEUTSCHLAND	Germany
DEUTSCH OSTAFRIKA	German East Africa
D'HAITI	Haiti
D'ITALIA	Italy
ERYTHR	Eritrea
ESPANA	Spain
FILIPINAS	Philippines
FOEDERATI BELGII	Netherlands
FRANCAISE	France
FUN	Korea
GHANIENSIS	Ghana
GOA	Portuguese India
GRONLAND	Greenland
GUINEE	Guinea
HELVETIA	Switzerland
HELVETICA	Switzerland
HIBERNIA	Ireland
HISPANIARUM	Spain
HOND	Honduras
HRVATSKA	Croatia
HVNGARIA	Hungary
ILES DE FRANCE ET BONAPARTE	Mauritius
ISLAND	Iceland
ITALIA	Italy
KATANGA	Congo
LATVIJAS	Latvia
LETZEBURG	Luxembourg
LIBANAISE	Lebanon
LIETUVAS	Lithuania
MAGYAR	Hungary
MAROC	Morocco

MEXICANA	Mexico
MILETA	Malta
MOCAMBIQUE	Mozambique
MONOEGA	Monaco
NEDERLANDEN	Netherlands
NORGE	Norway
NORVEG	Norway
NUEVA GRANADA	Colombia
OESTERREICH	Austria
OSTAFRIKANISCHE	German East Africa
OSTERREICH	Austria
PENNIA	Finland
POLSKIE	Poland
PORTUGUESA	Portugal
ROMANIA	Romania
SCOTORVM	Scotland
SHQIPERI	Albania
S. MARINO	San Marino
SOMALIS	French Somaliland
SUID AFRIKA	South Africa
SUOMEN	Finland
SURINAME	Surinam
SVERIGES	Sweden
SYRIE	Syria
TASAVALTA	Finland
TUNISIE	Tunisia
TURKIYE	Turkey
VATICANO	Vatican City
ZEELANDIA	Netherlands
ZEL	Netherlands
ZUID AFRIKA	South Africa

Modern Foreign Denominations

Here is a list of many of the nations in the world, along with the denominations of their *current* coinage system.

Afghanistan	afghani = 100 puls
Albania	lek = 100 qindarka
Algeria	franc = 100 centimes
Angola	escudo = 100 centavos
Argentina	peso = 100 centavos
Australia	pound = 20 schillings equals 240 pence

Austria	shilling = 100 groschen
Bahamas	dollar = 100 cents
Bahrain	denar = 1,000 fils
Belgian Congo	franc = 100 centimes
Belgium	franc = 100 centimes
Bolivia	boliviano = 100 centavos
Brazil	cruzeiro = 100 centavos
British Caribbean	
Territories	dollar = 100 cents
British Honduras	dollar = 100 cents
British West Africa	shilling = 12 pence
Bulgaria	lev = 100 stotinki
Burma	kyat = 100 pyas
Burundi	franc = 100 centimes
Canada	dollar = 100 cents
Cape Verde Islands	escudo = 100 centavos
Ceylon (Sri Lanka)	rupee = 100 cents
Chile	peso = 100 centavos
Cocos-Keeling	
Islands	rupee = 100 cents
Colombia	peso = 100 centavos
Comoro Islands	franc = 100 centimes
Costa Rica	colon = 100 centimes
Crete	drachma = 100 lepta
Cuba	peso = 100 centavos
Curacao	gulden = 100 cents
Cyprus	pound = 100 shillings
Czechoslovakia	koruna = 100 keller
Denmark	krone = 100 ore
Dominican Republic	peso = 100 centavos
East Africa	shilling = 100 cents
Ecuador	sucre = 100 centavos
Egypt	pound = 100 piastres = 1,000 milliemes
Eritrea	lira = 100 centesimi
Estonia	kroon = 100 marka
Ethiopia	dollar = 100 cents
Fiji	pound = 20 shillings = 240 pence
Finland	markka = 100 pennia
France	franc = 100 centimes
Gambia (The)	dalasi = 100 bututs
Germany	mark = 100 pfennigs
Ghana	cepi = 100 pesewas
Great Britain	pound = 100 new pence

Greece	drachma = 100 lepta
Greenland	krone = 100 ore
Guatemala	quetzal = 100 centavos
Guernsey	pound = 100 new pence
Haiti	gourde = 100 centimes
Honduras	lempira = 100 centavos
Hong Kong	dollar = 100 cents
Hungary	forint = 100 filler
Iceland	krona = 100 aurar
India	rupee = 100 naya paise
Indonesia	rupiah = 100 sen
Iran	rial = 100 dinars
Iraq	dinar = 5 riyals = 1,000 fils
Ireland	pound = 100 new pence
Israel	pound = 100 agorot
Italy	lira = 100 centesimi
Jamaica	dollar = 100 cents
Japan	yen = 100 sen
Jersey	pound = 100 new pence
Jordan	dinar = 1,000 fils
Kenya	shilling = 100 cents
Korea	won = 100 chon
Kuwait	dinar = 100 fils
Lebanon	pound = 100 piastres
Liberia	dollar = 100 cents
Libya	pound = 100 piastres = 1,000 mills
Liechtenstein	frank = 100 rappen
Luxembourg	franc = 100 centimes
Macao	pataca = 100 avos
Madagascar	franc = 100 centimes
Mauritius	rupee = 100 cents
Mexico	peso = 100 centavos
Monaco	franc = 100 centimes
Mongolia	tukhrik = 100 mongos
Morocco	franc = 100 centimes
Mozambique	escudo = 100 centavos
Muscat and Oman	saidi ryal = 1,000 baizah
Nepal	rupee = 100 paisa
Netherlands	gulden = 100 cents
Netherland Antilles	gulden = 100 cents
New Caledonia	franc = 100 centimes
New Zealand	dollar = 100 cents
Nicaragua	cordoba = 100 centavos

Nigeria	naira = 100 kobo
Norway	krone = 100 ore
Pakistan	rupee = 16 annas
Panama	balboa = 100 centesimos
Paraguay	guarani = 100 centimos
Peru	sol = 100 centavos
Philippines	peso = 100 centavos
Poland	zloty = 100 groszy
Portugal	escudo = 100 centavos
Portuguese Guinea	escudo = 100 centavos
Portuguese India	rupia = 16 tangas
Rhodesia	dollar = 100 cents
Romania	leu = 100 bani
Salvador	colon = 100 centavos
Saudi Arabia	ryal = 20 ghirsh
Seychelles	rupee = 100 cents
Somalia	somalo = 100 centesimi
South Africa	rand = 100 cents
Spain	peseta = 100 centimos
Sudan	ghirsh = 10 millim
Sweden	krona = 100 ore
Switzerland	franc = 100 centimes
Syria	pound = 100 piastres
Thailand	baht = 100 satangs
Tibet	srang = 10 sho
Timor	pataca = 100 avo
Togo	franc = 100 centimes
Tunisia	franc = 100 centimes
Turkey	lira = 100 kurus
Uruguay	peso = 100 centesimas
USSR	ruble = 100 kopecks
Vatican City	lira = 100 centesimi
Venezuela	bolivar = 100 centimas
Vietnam	dong = 100 xu
Yugoslavia	dinar = 100 paras

5. Tokens and Medals

What do the following three things have in common? A telephone call in Israel, a subway ride in New York, and the 1896 and 1900 presidential campaigns of William Jennings Bryan.

The answer is tokens. In Israel you must buy tokens at a post office in order to use any of the pay phones in the nation. In New York to ride the subway you must buy tokens at special booths in subway stations. The supporters of William Jennings Bryan issued political tokens, many of which were large silver pieces containing exactly one dollar's worth of silver. (A key campaign issue of the day was that the silver dollar contained only about half of the silver value of a gold dollar—412.5 grains as opposed to 823 grains.)

An Israeli telephone token.

A United States "Bryan token" with the inscriptions "Free Coinage, One Dime, 1897" and "From Silver Mines of Bunco State."

These are only three examples of tokens. There are, of course, many, many more. Tokens physically resemble coins, but are usually issued privately and do not have any official government status as legal tender. Sometimes, however, tokens will do the work of ordinary coins. In other instances the use of tokens may be limited; for example, they may be redeemable only for goods at certain merchants, or for specific services.

Tokens have been used to gain publicity in political campaigns, as advertising devices, as tickets of admission, or as chits that permit a subway or streetcar ride or a telephone call.

Among the earliest tokens are the ancient tesserae (singular, "tessera") made of lead or bronze and used by the Romans as gifts which allowed the recipients a certain amount of food or money. At other times in the ancient world these "tessies" were used as admission tickets to the theater or circus.

The tesserae were often given out to the people on special occasions, such as on the emperor's birthday or the time of his accession to the throne.

Tokens have often come into being because of a shortage of small change in a particular nation or region. In sixteenth-century England, for example, the growth of trade caused a considerable shortage of small change, and base-metal tokens circulated widely to help alleviate this shortage. Some of the tokens were struck by local traders themselves, a tradition that continued for centuries.

Similar situations have arisen throughout history, even very recently. In the United States in about 1975 the price of copper jumped to the point where the copper value of the 1-cent coin practically exceeded the nominal value of the coin. People began to hoard the cents, and the mint could not produce them quickly enough. As a result many merchants could not provide the proper change to their customers, and many of them printed 1-cent chits, redeemable at a later time. By this time, the value of 1 cent had become so small that few problems were actually caused, and in some stores customers were perfectly happy to round off their bills to the nearest nickel. But in earlier days similar shortages caused more serious problems.

In England more than twenty thousand different types of tokens were issued between 1648 and 1672. These tokens had no legal-tender status, but were officially sanctioned, since James I and Charles I granted the rights to issue them as patronage. The crown, of course, reserved the right to issue coins in silver and gold, but the king's lack of interest in issuing coins of the common base metals caused a severe shortage of small change. Unfortunately the privilege of issuing base-metal tokens was granted to a few who grossly abused it, and when these individuals refused to redeem the tokens as promised there were many problems. During this time other tokens were issued by municipalities, merchants, and especially taverns. Often the tokens circulated only within a few blocks of the tavern that issued them.

In 1672, Charles II issued the first official British copper coins and prohibited the issue of private tokens. But before too long (between 1755 and 1769), England again stopped striking regal copper coins. From 1770 to 1775 a few halfpennies and farthings (quarter-pennies) were issued, but there were too few to make any difference, and a desperate need for minor currency again arose in England. This set off a major wave of eighteenth-century British tokens. Many of these tokens doubled as prestigious advertisements for the merchants who issued them. Others were overtly political in nature. Some of the political tokens were issued by bookseller and avowed revolutionary Thomas Spence. One of his tokens announced: "Thos. Spence, Sir Thos. More, Thos. Paine, Noted advocates for the rights of man." Another Spence token proclaimed: "If rents I once consent to pay my liberty is fast away." And on the reverse a boar is shown trampling on symbols of royalty.

These radicals, of course, weren't the only ones to get their licks in, and their tokens were often promptly answered by conservative-issued pieces. One of these showed three men (obviously the three mentioned above) being hanged, with the legend: "Noted Advocates for the rights of man," and on the reverse the phrase: "A way to prevent knaves getting a trick."

These British tokens, and many other varieties, can still be found in quite excellent condition for only a few dollars. They are an interesting area for further study.

United States Tokens

There have been a large number of tokens issued in the United States in various categories. In 1915 Thomas L. Elder read a paper to the New York Numismatic Club in which he explained, "Tokens portray national, local, political, commercial and personal history. They record many of the quaint slogans and political sayings of the times; they often bear the portraits of noted men and women, or advertise the various classes of goods handled by the American merchant. On them we observe the foibles and fashions of the time, and their workmanship furnishes us with a fair guide to the artistic taste of the day."

That description might hold true for the tokens of other nations as well, but Elder was describing the tokens of the United States. American tokens were issued for the same basic reasons as tokens were issued in England and elsewhere.

Two of the major categories of United States tokens are Hard Times tokens and Civil War tokens. There are many others and many varieties of these types.

The Hard Times tokens of bronze, copper, brass, other metals, and even hard fibrous materials were issued from about 1832 to 1844, and many were especially related to the financial panic of 1837. They served to alleviate a severe shortage of small change, just as they had in England three centuries before. The Hard Times tokens were the first United States tokens used in commerce to any significant degree, even though there are records of tokens being used in the Colonies since 1714.

As most series of circulating tokens, the Hard Times tokens are both commercial and political in nature, each group having special attractions for collectors. The political tokens mainly related to the controversial President Andrew Jackson, who refused to recharter the Bank of the United States. Other "politicals" aimed at slavery, the protective tariff during the War of 1812, the silver versus gold question, and other controversial matters of the day. The commercial American tokens in this or other periods are generally known as U.S. store cards or merchant's tokens.

These store cards were not only advertising "cards" but also apparently made money for the merchants as well. Thomas Elder noted, "It is of interest . . . that H. M. and E. I. Richards, of Attleboro, Mass., sold their tokens by the keg-full to their customers for from 60 to 75 cents per hundred."

They were obviously making a profit if they could afford to sell them at a 25 to 40 percent discount in quantity. They must have figured that a good percentage of their tokens would never be redeemed, hence they could come out ahead. Judging from the popularity of the large cent-sized tokens among merchants, they must have done just that!

The tokens of this period in American history were catalogued by Lyman H. Low, and published in 1899. As Low and others who have described their history note, the tokens are a genuine mirror of the times. Low and others who have written a lot about tokens seem to go a step beyond the usual, and into the stories of the individuals who ordered the issues.

One fascinating store card shows on the obverse the inscription "PHALONS NEW & SPLENDID STYLE OF HAIR CUTTING," and on the reverse a pair of scissors, a comb, the address "No. 35 BOWERY, NEW YORK," and the date, 1837.

Of this token Low writes: "Edward Phalon probably began his business as hair-dresser at 161 Chatham Street in 1834; from that date until 1860 his change of location occurred at least eleven times, among them being that to the Bowery, indicated on the token. In 1842 he was opposite St. Paul's, at 214 Broadway, where he sold the 'Amazon Toupee,' for which and for his 'Wigs and Scalps' the American Institute awarded him a silver medal in 1841, and the first premium in 1842. In 1848 . . . he advertised extensively a famous 'Chemical Hair Invigorator.' The height of his prosperity was reached when, after several other removals, he occupied a gorgeous shop in the St. Nicholas Hotel, where the prices charged for service and for the various cosmetics which he offered for sale, were in accordance with the brilliancy of the numerous mirrors, the gilded frames, the marble basins, and their silver-plated fixtures, which adorned the place. . . . I had a pleasant interview with him in 1886, though he could give me little information about his card."

Among other store cards issued are those advertising "John J. Adams of Taunton, Mass." The Adams firm, according to the obverse of its token, specialized in "All kinds of brushes, Made to order," and featured a boar design. Robinson's, Jones & Co., of New York, wanted to let it be known that one should patronize them "For the best military, naval, sporting and plain flat buttons." W.A. Handy, a "Merchant Tailor," of Providence, R.I., also issued tokens in this period.

Many of the political tokens were satirical, especially at the expense of President Jackson, known to his enemies as a "tyrant," and a very stubborn man. Hence the jackass is one of the favorite symbols depicting him.

One of these coins shows on the obverse the legend "A PLAIN SYSTEM VOID OF POMP," with Jackson advancing left with a sword in his right hand and a purse in his left hand. The reverse carries "THE CONSTITUTION AS I UNDERSTAND IT," and a balking mule fac-

Three United States Hard Times tokens.

ing right. On the mule are the letters "LL.D." and above it, "ROMAN FIRMNESS," with the date 1834.

The mule with the title "LL.D." on it recalls the honorary Doctorate of Laws degree that Harvard College gave Jackson in 1833. Low notes that the college had "desired to honor the patriotic soldier who was the President of the United States and the defender of the Union, but who was no scholar, and who had resigned his seat in the Senate because he felt out of place in 'so slow and dignified a body,' the judicious grieved, and his enemies rejoiced at the absurdity of the title . . ."

As to the rest of the token, Low writes, "The quotation 'A plain system' etc., is a sharp satire on the professed Jeffersonian Democracy of Jackson. In his speeches and public documents he was constantly upholding the doctrines of the third president, who was 'the very embodiment of democracy,' and to whom all titles of honor, even that of Mr., were distasteful, who dressed in the plainest style, and whose Inauguration was pre-eminently 'void of pomp'; but the brilliant war record of Jackson was ever on the lips of his party followers. Somewhat egotistic in his way of expressing himself, due rather to his sense of the dignity and powers of his high office than to any great personal vanity, the satirists delighted to portray him in a dress suit awkwardly brandishing his weapon, or in full uniform as a General, with epaulets and sword, and all of the 'pomp' of war, with 'MY glory,' or some similar phrase added . . ."

Another political token of the day carried the obverse inscription "SUBSTITUTE FOR SHIN PLASTERS" around a phoenix rising from flames and the date 1837. The reverse shows a wreath and the inscription "MILLIONS FOR DEFENCE NOT ONE CENT FOR TRIBUTE."

"Shin plasters" is the name that was applied to bills issued by irresponsible banks and private parties at the time. "The device of the phoenix rising from the flames seems to mean that the paper money was only fit to be burned, and that with its destruction new life would spring from its ashes," Low explained.

Another interesting group of 1-cent and 3-cent tokens were issued by Dr. Lewis Feuchtwanger, merchant, metallurgist, and doctor. His major claims to fame are the gray metal alloy he invented and the Feuchtwanger cents, which became, in size at least, prototypes for the Flying Eagle cents, and are roughly the same size as cents used today.

Of Feuchtwanger, Low writes: "Dr. Lewis Feuchtwanger's first business location appears to have been at 377 Broadway, where he remained from 1831 to 1837; thereafter, until 1857, his changes were numerous, and, considering the limits of the city within that period, he may be said to have roved widely. He is given in the Directories twelve different addresses, ranging from No. 1 Wall Street to 21 White Street, three of which are in Maiden Lane. He was the inventor of an alloyed metal, resembling 'German Silver' which he hoped to induce the government to adopt for minor coinage. He was a druggist and chemist, and in 1832 in addition to this business he also sold natural curiosities, such as rare minerals, gems, preserved reptiles, etc., a large collection of which he placed on exhibition at Peale's Museum, and the 'New York Lyceum of Natural History.' At his Broadway store, 'one door below White Street,' he advertised 'Nurembergh Salve' and 'Kreosote . . . a recent German discovery for preventing tooth-ache!' These nostrums seem to have been highly esteemed in their time."

From 1861 to 1864, merchants of more than three hundred towns in twenty-three states issued Civil War tokens, again because of a shortage of small change. This time the shortage occurred because of the war and fear of devaluation; metallic currency began to disappear from circulation and be hoarded away. The Civil War tokens are often struck in a general imitation of the Indian Head cents, and were struck in any number of base metals and occasionally in silver. More than 8,500 different types of store cards and more than 1,500 types of political tokens were struck during this period. The total issue of tokens of Civil War vintage was more than 25 million! Among the patriotic tokens are those with inscriptions such as "OUR LITTLE MONITOR," "TERRORS OF WAR—BLESSINGS OF PEACE," "RHODE ISLAND—FIRST IN THE FIELD," and, referring to the American flag, "IF ANYONE ATTEMPTS TO TEAR IT DOWN SHOOT HIM ON THE SPOT" (an error version of the same piece has "ON THE SPOOT").

Five Civil War tokens.

Encased postage stamp advertising Ayer's Pills.

In 1862, John Gault patented an encasing for postage stamps. These metal frames held the stamps, which were covered by a piece of mica to protect the stamp from the wear and tear of circulation. Merchant ads were usually embossed on the metal side. These encased stamps were used in place of small change.

Transportation tokens, gambling tokens, fraternal tokens, and even bawdy-house tokens are among those that have also been issued in the United States. Some enthusiasts collect only transportation tokens, others may collect tokens from various casinos. Coin dealer Q. David Bowers writes that he has "collected . . . many different tokens—mostly the size of a nickel—once used to operate electric pianos (nickelodeons) and orchestrions, the automatic self-playing orchestras."

Token collecting is a fascinating and potentially diverse branch of numismatics which offers the collector an unusual chance to carry out some original research into the individual, firm, or group that issued particular pieces.

Medals

The poet Goethe observed, "A daily pastime worthy of a man's adoption would be the contemplation of a few medals."

Here we are not referring specifically to military medals or decorations, but to the usually round objects that often look like large coins. A medal is a commemorative object, to recall a person, place, or event, made either at the time or later.

Thus medals are a mirror of contemporary life and taste, often preserving the likeness of famous persons. It is also common for the images and inscriptions on the reverse of medals to describe the achievements of these persons.

Medals differ from coins in the sense that they were not intended as a medium of exchange, but only as commemorative pieces. Indeed, medal collectors will tell you that the size, technique, and

Inaugural medal for Franklin Roosevelt and John Nance Garner.

Nineteenth-century medal commemorating John Adams.

Papal States medal commemorating Innocent XI (Odeschalchi), pope from 1676 to 1689. The reverse shows Jesus giving the keys of Heaven to St. Peter.

officialness of the medal are not the heart of the matter. The person or event being commemorated is the important thing.

The first medals were struck under the Roman emperors as rewards or gifts. This custom faded out with the decline of Rome's glory, but was revived with great enthusiasm during the Renaissance, about the middle of the fifteenth century.

The creator of the modern medal was Antonio Pisano, called Pisanello. He was born in 1397 in Verona, and died in 1455. Pisanello was forty-two when he created his first medal. He often depicted marvelous animals, which reflected his great artistic skills.

By the sixteenth century, with the development of improved methods of striking, an increased number of medals were produced. These were reserved for the upper classes, and they didn't hesitate to use them for their own self-glorification.

Over the next few hundred years the process of manufacturing medals became even less expensive, and thus increasingly accessible to the upward-striving middle class. An increasing number of wealthy merchants had themselves commemorated on medals, which they commissioned.

In the nineteenth century there was again a tremendous increase in the numbers of medals being made. This was largely due to mechanization in the form of both the steam press and the reducing machine, which spared the artist the pains of carefully engraving a tiny, unique die.

Ever since the beginning of modern medal making in the fifteenth century, there has been an air of commercialism around many medals. Medals were, in other words, often manufactured *to sell* to people. The ultimate extension of this practice is the many private mints operating today which strike hundreds of medals every year just for collectors to purchase. This practice has cheapened the field of medal collecting, for the genuine medals of their day can rarely be surpassed in both beauty and historical significance.

Among a few of the categories that some medal collectors specialize are: Medals concerning the place you live; religious medals; medals dealing with medicine; satirical medals; anti-Semitic medals; and medals commemorating men of the arts and letters, architects, musicians, composers, aviators, and politicians.

6. Ancient Coins

My own greatest collecting pleasure is in the field of ancient coins. These small bits of metal were used by people as long as 2,500 years ago, and to me this is one of the most exciting aspects of numismatics.

The ancient coins frighten away many beginners because at first glance they are so "different" from the coins that circulate today. In fact, there are more similarities between modern and ancient coins than there are differences. Nevertheless, the unusual shape, thickness, uneven and often ragged appearance, and the strange style and design are frequently sufficient to frighten away the potential new collector.

Dekadrachm of Syracuse, said to be one of the most beautiful coins ever struck.

The opposite should actually occur. In fact, it was long a coin-collecting maxim that the beginner ought to start collecting the ancient series to help whet his appetite for knowledge, and to impose discipline on his collecting habits.

In the preface to his 1959 book *An Outline of Ancient Greek Coins*, Zander Klawans writes; "If my reader intends to begin this hobby with a speculative eye, I shall now warn him to look elsewhere. As in all coinage, ancient coinage has appreciated in value, but slowly enough so as to make the coins unprofitable in any monetary sense. One must be prepared to take a different kind of profit . . . that of the spirit."

Klawan's last sentence is still true, of course. This "spiritual profit" is often the most rewarding. However, the ancient coin market has been booming for nearly a decade. After stratospheric highs in the mid-1970s, the market for ancient coins has once again calmed a bit, but there are still substantial jumps in price with some degree of regularity.

Thus one might say that the ancient coin series are no better and no worse as investments than other series of government-issued coins. One difference, however, is that there will never again be these types of coins struck—anywhere in the world. At the same time, however, many dozens of governments continue to issue extensions of their existing series of modern coins.

The collector of ancient coins could specialize in any number of areas. In this brief chapter only some of the major areas of specialization in ancient coins will be discussed—the Greek coins, the Roman coins, and the coins of the Byzantine Empire. Coins of Bible days are the subject of the next chapter.

Ancient Greek Coins

This series is not limited only to those coins issued in ancient Greece, but consists of all coins issued throughout the ancient Greek world—which ranged from Spain to Carthage and from Egypt to Greece as well as throughout the Greek islands. All in all more than a thousand Greek city-states throughout the world issued coins. The armies of the ancient Greeks were not strangers to any of the areas surrounding the Mediterranean.

The ancient Greek world ranged from Carthage (top) to Egypt (below) and beyond, as shown by these two coins.

There are generally said to be seven periods of Greek art. The art of the coin styles also falls roughly into these periods, but they are not indicative of particular dating systems:

1. Archaic art—700–480 B.C.
2. Transitional art—480–415 B.C.
3. Finest art—415–336 B.C.
4. Later fine art—336–280 B.C.
5. Decline of art—280–146 B.C.
6. Continued decline in art—146–27 B.C.
7. Imperial period—27 B.C.–296 A.D.

If it hasn't already struck you from looking at the pictures of the ancient coins on these pages, you should take note that there are actually no conventional "dates" on any of the ancient coins. Obviously, in the years now known as B.C., the people living had no way of knowing that years would eventually be designated in this way. The same was true for the first decades following the death of Jesus. The fact is that the first coins using our current dating system were not struck until the year 1234 by the Roskilde mint, now in Denmark. By that time coins had been minted for more than 1,500 years. Many of those prior coins had dates, but they were not dates as we know them today. Ancient coins were dated by the regnal year of the ruler, or by some kind of local era.

This would be the equivalent of 1978 coins of the United States being dated "Year Two," meaning "The second year of the rule of Jimmy Carter."

All ancient eras are not linked to the rulers, however, and various other events often mark their starts. Great victories, visits of an emperor to a particular town, and other major events are a few examples.

DENOMINATIONS OF GREEK COINS

Various areas within the Greek empire adopted their own "standards" or units for the weights of coins. There were six major weight standards: Attic, Aeginetic, Phoenician, Rhodian, Babylonic, and Persic. These standards were quite probably all derived from an ancient Babylonian standard of weight, the *manah*, discovered by Sir Henry Layard of the British Museum, who excavated the site of the ancient city of Nineveh. He discovered various weights, some in the form of ducks and others in the form of lions. From inscriptions on them, and a lot of computations, archaeologists and numismatists have figured the approximate equivalents in the various standards. While the differences between the standards are significant, just as important for you to understand are the relationships between the different denominations of the ancient Greek coins. These are all denominations of silver coins. Gold coins were rarely issued in ancient Greece, and the relative values of the bronze coins are somewhat vague.

Coin	Equivalent
Dekadrachm	10 drachms
Tetradrachm	4 drachms
Didrachm	2 drachms
Drachm	6 obols
Tetrobol	4 obols
Triobol or hemidrachm	3 obols or ½ drachm
Diobol	2 obols
Obol	1/6 drachm
Tritemorion	¾ obol
Hemiobol	½ obol
Trihemitartemorion	⅜ obol
Tetartemorion	¼ obol
Hemitartemorion	⅛ obol

Tetradrachm of Athens (131–130 B.C.*).*

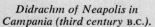

Didrachm of Neapolis in Campania (third century B.C.*).*

Drachm of Epidamnus Dyrrachachium in Illyricum (third century B.C.*).*

Some of the latter denominations are so tiny that it is a wonder that any of them have survived—yet they have, often in excellent condition.

TYPES OF GREEK COINS

It would take many pages to discuss all of the various city-states of ancient Greece that issued coins, and it would take many volumes to describe even a portion of the coins that each of them issued. The British Museum Catalogue of Greek Coins is made up of twenty-nine sizable volumes, and there are many thousands of ancient Greek coins that are not described. This series of coins, in fact, is so extensive that some advanced collectors must have libraries containing thousands of books, magazines, and sale catalogues. Some of these libraries are worth more than $100,000. The true numismatic scholars perceive that their libraries are just as important as, or even more important than, their coins.

There are hundreds of interesting coin types of the ancient Greek empire. Many of the city-states issued coins with insignia that became city symbols. Athens issued an extensive series of coins with the famous Athenian owl, Rhodian coins often carried the famous rose of Rhodes, coins of Corinth depicted the winged horse Pegasus, coins of Aegina often showed a turtle, coins of Ephesus depicted the bee, coins of Thurium portrayed a bull, ears of wheat appeared on coins of Metapontum, and a characteristic shield was stamped on the coins of Boetia.

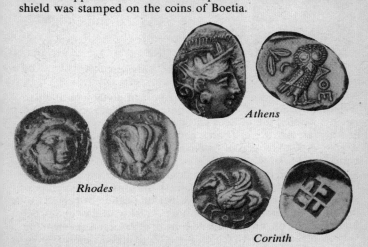

Athens

Rhodes

Corinth

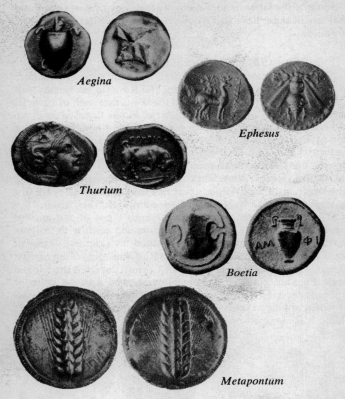

Aegina

Ephesus

Thurium

Boetia

Metapontum

The Greek coins also carried a plethora of mythological types, including lovely depictions of Aphrodite, goddess of love and beauty; Apollo, son of Zeus and the sun god; Ares, or Mars, the god of war; Artemis or Diana, goddess of the chase and sister of Apollo; Asklepios, god of medicine and healing; Athena or Minerva, goddess of wisdom; Demeter or Ceres, goddess of fertility, agriculture, and marriage; Dionysos or Bacchus, god of the vine; the Dioscuri twins (Castor and Pollux), the sons of Zeus and protectors of travelers; Eirene or Pax, personification of peace; Euthenia or Abundantia, personification of plenty; Helios or Sol, the sun god; Hera or Juno, sister and consort of Zeus and queen of the heavens; Herakles or Hercules, son of Zeus and the most famous mythological hero; Hygieia, goddess of health; Nike, Greek goddess of victory; Pan, god of shepherds and flocks; Poseidon or Neptune, ruler of the sea; and Zeus or Jupiter, the father of both gods and men.

Athena on a tetradrachm of Ptolemy I of Egypt (323–284 B.C.).

Nike on a plated tetradrachm of Gallienus struck in Alexandria.

Zeus on a tetradrachm of Alexander II of Syria (128–123 B.C.).

These are but a few of the fascinating types to be found on ancient Greek coins. Barclay Head has made an important observation: "All through the history of free and independent Greece, and even until the death of Alexander the Great, the main object of the coin-type was to place before the people an ideal representation of the divinity most honoured in the district in which the coin was intended to circulate. No tyrant, however despotic, no general, however splendid in his achievements by land or sea, no demagogue, however inflated his vanity, ever sought to perpetuate his features on the current coin. Hence the mythological interest of the coin-types is paramount, from the first introduction of the art of coining down to the age of the successors of Alexander."

The various series of portrait coins of ancient Greek rulers begins only after 323 B.C., the year of the death of Alexander the Great. Even he did not order his image placed upon coins, but used the bust of Herakles, his patron god.

Alexander's death also marked the beginning of the downfall of the Greek empire itself, which Alexander's strength had held together. On Alexander's death the empire was divided among several of the Macedonian generals who had fought under him during his march through Asia.

Alexander the Great

Ptolemy I

Portrait coin of Lysimachus of Thrace.

A large part of the eastern portion of the empire went to his general Antigonus. Seleucis built a mighty empire stretching from Syria to the borders of India. Lysimachus, who had been commander of Alexander's bodyguard, became ruler of Thrace, a province in the north of Greece. Another of Alexander's great generals was Ptolemy, who held and enlarged Egypt as his share of his former ruler's empire.

Several of these former generals issued coins with portraits of

Alexander himself. His successors no doubt did this to help identify themselves, in the minds of the people, with the powerful Alexander. Soon various rulers began to have their own portraits engraved and struck upon the coins issued in their territories. Ptolemy became the first living person to have his image stamped upon coins just after he assumed the title of king in 305 B.C. That same portrait was reproduced on coins struck by Ptolemy's successors for about three centuries.

Continued dissension and bickering among the various Greek rulers further weakened, and eventually destroyed, the empire. Even as early as the third century B.C., Rome had begun her climb to the pinnacle of power in the ancient world.

By 148 B.C., Macedon herself had given in to the Romans, and from that time forward Macedon, and most of the other Greek city-states, were simply provinces of the mighty Roman Empire. This is reflected in the series of coins known as Greek Imperials, since they were struck at the local mints of the former Greek colonies, but were now issued under the authority of the reigning Roman emperor. Hence these frequently carry an imperial portrait on the obverse, and some kind of a local mythological or city scene on the reverse.

Roman Coins

The earliest Roman coins were very large cast bronze pieces— some almost the size of a fist. They were known as *aes grave*. They were first issued by the Roman Republic about 269 B.C. At about the same time the Romans also issued smaller struck bronze coins, as well as silver pieces. The bronze coins were issued in denominations known as the *as, semis, triens, quadrans, sextans,* and *uncia.* The early silver pieces were didrachms and the quadrigatus, and later the victoriatus.

Huge cast coin of the Roman Republic (222–205 B.C.), called aes grave.

In 187 B.C. the classic denomination of ancient Roman coinage, the denarius, was introduced. It was later known as the silver penny, and the abbreviation "1 d." eventually became the abbreviation for the British penny. Fractions of the early denarii were also issued in the forms of the quinarius (half) and the silver sestertius (quarter).

When the procession of Roman emperors began, gold, too, became a metal of regularly issued coins and the revised list of denominations of Roman coins was as follows:

Coin	Equivalent
Gold aureus	25 silver denarii
AR denarius	16 AE asses
AR quinarius	8 AE asses
AE sestertius	4 AE asses
AE dupondius	2 AE asses
AE as	4 AE quadrantes
AE semis	2 AE quadrantes
AE quadrans	¼ AE as

Denarius of Trajan   *Quinarius of Augustus*

Sestertius of Nero

Dupondius of Hadrian

As of Nero

Antoninianus of Philip I

The dupondius and the as were often similar in size and design, the main distinction being that the dupondius was often struck of the yellowish alloy called orichalcum, while the as was struck of reddish copper. The later dupondii also carry busts of the emperor with the radiate crown, while portraits on the as usually carried the laureate wreath.

Still later another denomination, the antoninianus, was issued, and came to replace the denarius. The antoninianus was a base silver coin worth about 1 ½ denarii. With each crisis of the empire the antoninianus was more and more debased, and eventually, under Valerian in 260 A.D., it was reduced to a bronze coin with a thin silver wash. Now, too, the normal brass and copper coins were no longer issued, and gold coins were struck only to pay the troops. By the reign of Diocletian (284-304) a complete reform was made in the system of coinage in 296. His main task was to re-purify the coinage and introduce new, reliable denominations. The follis was a new bronze coin, with a silver wash, and now 1 gold aureus equaled 20 silver argenti equaled 40 folles.

Silqua of Valens

The follis quickly began to decline in both size and weight, and in 312, Constantine the Great again had to reorganize the coinage. Constantine's system was based on the golden solidus, seventy-two of which were made from each pound of gold. The silver siliqua was 1/24 of a solidus. Later there were also other denominations, including the silver miliarense, 1/14 of a solidus; and the gold semissis (half-solidus) and tremissis (third-solidus). Bronze coins also continued declining in size and weight, and today these later pieces are known only according to their relative sizes, that is (from largest to smallest), AE1, AE2, AE3, and AE4.

COLLECTING CATEGORIES OF ROMAN COINS

It is the intention of many collectors to assemble complete sets of one portrait coin for each of the Roman emperors. Others choose to build type sets of denominations, and still other collectors fancy the interesting reverse types. David Sear's classic *Roman Coins and Their Values* lists several categories of reverse types on Roman coins:

- Deities and personifications
- Representations of the emperor and his family
- Types of military conquest and victories
- Legionary types
- Geographical types
- Architectural types
- Animals
- Posthumous types

There are also series of Roman coins with reverse types, including heavenly bodies, inscriptions, mythological types, nautical types, and symbolic types.

The photographs on these pages show but a few of the fascinating reverse types of Roman coins. As for the Greek series, many thousands of volumes have been published simply cataloguing the tens of thousands of different issues.

IDENTIFYING ROMAN COINS

The Roman coins are far easier to identify than the Greek pieces, which come from so many different city-states. It is also relatively simple to decipher the inscriptions on the Roman pieces, though the task may seem difficult to the beginner. Who would feel comfortable deciphering a legend like "IMPCAESVESPASIANAVGPMTRPPPPCOSIII" for the first time?

This legend gives us not only the name of the emperor, but his titles, and the date of issue of the coin as well.

Let's break down the legend to make it a bit more palatable: IMP CAES VESPASIAN AVG PM TR P P P COS III. Unfortunately those breaks between words and abbreviations usually don't occur on the coins. Here is what this inscription means. From this example you'll have a good start on other inscriptions.

IMP—short for *Imperator*, or emperor

CAES—short for *Caesar*, a family name and title adopted by the Roman emperors

VESPASIAN—the name of the emperor himself

AVG—*Augustus*, the distinctive imperial title, used by no other than the reigning emperor or immediate family members

PM—*Pontifex Maximus*, a common imperial title which literally means "head priest," referring to the emperor as supreme head of the Roman religion

TR P—*Tribunicia Potestate*, or the tribunician power, which represents the emperor as the representative of the people, or the highest civil authority of the state. Often a series of numerals will follow the TR P, such as TR P IIII, or TR P X, which refer to particular years and thus can be used to date coins. In the case of Vespasian this refers to the year 69 A.D.

PP—*Pater Patriae*, or father of his country

COS III—in his third consulship. There were two chief magistrates of the Roman state; the emperor was usually one of them. The consulships lasted for only a year, and were then renewed or transferred, thus the numeral following a consulship can also signify a date. In the case of Vespasian, COS III refers to the year 71 A.D.

Many of the names of the Roman emperors are not as easy to identify as that of Vespasian. Here is an *abbreviated* list of some of the Roman emperors and other family members who issued coins, with their names as they often appear on the coins. (Many varieties of these names occur, so more detailed sources must be reviewed for specific information.)

Person	Dates	Name often appearing on coins
Julius Caesar	d. 44 B.C.	CAESAR
Mark Antony	d. 30 B.C.	M. ANTONIVS
Augustus	27 B.C.–14 A.D.	·AVGVSTVS
Tiberius	14–37 A.D.	TI CAESAR AVGVST
Caligula	37–41 A.D.	C CAESAR AVG GERMANICVS
Claudius	41–54	T CLAVD CAESAR

Person	Dates	Name often appearing on coins
Nero	54-68	NERO CAESAR AVG, NERO CLAVDIVS CAESAR
Clodius Macer	68	L CLODI MACRI

Galba	68–69	SER GALBA IMP
Otho	69	IMP OTHO CAESAR
Vitellius	69	A VITELLIVS GERMAN

Vespasian	69–79	IMP CAES VESPASIAN
Titus	79–81	T CAESAR VESPASIAN

Person	Dates	Name often appearing on coins
Domitian	81–96	IMP CAES DOMITIAN
Nerva	96–98	IMP NERVA CAES
Trajan	98–117	IMP CAES NERVA TRAIAN
Hadrian	117–138	IMP CAESAR TRAIAN HADRIANVS
Antoninus Pius	138–161	ANTONINVS AVG PIVS
Marcus Aurelius	161–180	AVRELIVS CAESAR AVG
Lucius Verus	161–169	L VERVS AVG
Commodus	177–192	L AVREL COMMODVS AVG, M COMMODVS ANT
Pertinax	193	IMP CAES P HELV PERTINAX

Person	Dates	Name often appearing on coins
Didius Julianus	193	IMP CAES M DID IVLIAN
Pescennius Niger	193–194	IMP CAES C PESC NIGER IVST
Clodius Albinus	195–197	D CLODIVS ALBINVS CAES

Septimius Severus	193–211	SEVERVS PIVS, IMP CAE L SEP SEV PERT AVG

Caracalla	198–217	ANTONINVS PIVS AVG
Geta	209–212	P SEPTIMIVS GETA PIVS AVG
Macrinus	217–218	IMP C M OPEL SEV MACRINVS AVG
Diadumenian	218	M OPEL ANT DIADVMENIAN

Elagabalus	218–222	IMP ANTONINVS PIVS AVG
Severus Alexander	222–235	IMP SEV ALEXANDER AVG

Person	Dates	Name often appearing on coins
Maximinus I	235–238	MAXIMINVS PIVS AVG
Gordian I	238	IMP CAES M ANT GORDIANVS AFR
Gordian II	238	IMP CAES M ANT GORDIANVS AFR
Balbinus	238	IMP CAES D CAEL BALBINVS AVG
Pupienus	238	IMP CAES M CLOD PVPIENVS AVG
Gordian III	238–244	IMP CAES GORDIANVS PIVS AVG
Philip I	244–249	IMP PHILIPPVS AVG
Philip II	247–249	M IVL PHILIPPVS
Trajan Decius	249–251	IMP C M Q TRAIANVS DECIVS
Hostilian	251	IMP CAE C VAL HOS MES QVINTVS

Person	Dates	Name often appearing on coins
Trebonianus Gallus	251–253	IMP CAE C VIB TREB GALLVS
Volusian	251–253	C VIBIO VOLVSIANO
Valerian I	253–260	IMP C P LIC VALERIANVS
Gallienus	253–268	GALLIENVS P F AVG
Quietus	260–261	IMP C FVL QVIETVS P F AVG

Person	Dates	Name often appearing on coins
Postumus	259–268	IMP C POSTVMVS P F AVG

Person	Dates	Name often appearing on coins
Victorinus	268–270	IMP C VICTORINVS P F AVG
Tetricus	270–273	IMP C TETRICVS P F AVG
Claudius II Gothicus	268–270	IMP C CLAVDIVS AVG
Aurelian	270–275	IMP C AVRELIANVS AVG
Tacitus	275–276	IMP C M CL TACITVS AVG
Probus	276–282	IMP C PROBVS P F AVG
Carus	282–283	IMP C M AVR CARVS P F AVG
Numerian	283–284	IMP NVMERIANVS
Carinus	283–285	M AVR CARINVS NOB

| Diocletian | 284–305 | IMP DIOCLETIANVS |

| Maximianus | 286–310 | IMP MAXIMIANVS |

Person	Dates	Name often appearing on coins

| Constantius I | 305–306 | IMP CONSTANTIVS |
| Gallerius | 305–311 | IMP C GAL VAL MAXIMIANVS |

| Maximinus II | 309–313 | IMP C GALER VAL MAXIMINVS |
| Maxentius | 306–312 | IMP C MAXENTIVS |

| Licinius I | 308–324 | IMP C LIC LICINNIVS |

Constantine I	307–337	IMP CONSTANTINVS
Constans	337–350	FL IVL CONSTANS
Magnentius	350–353	IMP CAE MAGNENTIVS

Person	Dates	Name often appearing on coins
Constantius Gallus	351–354	D N CONSTANTIVS IVN
Julian II	360–363	FL CL IVLIANVS
Jovian	363–364	D N IOVIANVS
Valentinian I	364–375	D N VALENTINIANVS
Valens	364–378	D N VALENS
Gratian	367–383	D N GRATIANVS

Valentinian II	375–392	D N VALENTINIANVS
Theodosius	379–395	D N THEODOSIVS
Magnus Maximus	383–388	D N MAG MAXIMVS
Arcadius	383–408	D N ARCADIVS
Honorius	393–423	D N HONORIVS
Theodosius II	402–450	D N THEODOSIVS

Byzantine Coins

The Roman Empire was split between the sons of Theodosius in 395. Honorius ruled the Western Empire from Rome, while Arcadius ruled the Eastern Empire from Constantinople.

Gradually the mints of the Western Empire fell into the hands of barbarians, and in 476, Romulus Augustulus, the last emperor, was deposed. But the Eastern Empire—the Byzantine Empire—continued for nearly a millennium, and preserved at least a part of the great Graeco-Roman civilization. The Byzantine Empire was held together until the fall of Constantinople in 1453. The empire was consolidated, and the coinage was reformed under Anastasius I (491–518).

The coins of the Byzantine Empire are generally less beautiful than those of Greece or Rome, and they are more crudely made. Nevertheless there is a lot of interest in this series because of the empire's role in the rise of Christendom. Many religious motifs are found on the Byzantine coins, and legends such as "SERVVS

Byzantine Empire, bronze follis of Justinian I (540–541 A.D.).

CHRISTI" ("Servant of Christ") and "CHRISTOS REX REGNANTIUM" (Christ, King of Kings) are frequently found on Byzantine coins, as are portrayals of Jesus himself.

The basic denominations of coins in the Byzantine Empire also changed from the earlier Roman standard. Perhaps the most famous Byzantine coin denomination was the golden solidus, used primarily to pay the army's wages. It may have been the name of this coin that gave rise to the use of the word "soldier" for those fighting men.

Here are the Byzantine Empire's common coin denominations:

Coin	Equivalent
Gold	
Solidus	24 AR siliqua
Semissis	12 AR siliqua
Tremissis	8 AR siliqua
Silver	
Miliarense	2 AR siliqua
Siliqua	300 AE nummi
Copper	
Follis	40 AE nummi
Nummus	1/7,200 AU solidus

7. Coins of the Holy Land

One of the most fascinating areas of numismatic study—and my own specialty—is the money of the Holy Land. Through these coins one can trace the rise of Judaism and Christianity, and even confirm many accounts of ancient history, both in the Bible and as quoted by ancient historians.

Coins of the Bible

The earliest known mention of money in the Bible is in the Old Testament story of Abraham. Among other items it speaks of silver with regard to the covenant of circumcision. Later in this same story we read the word "shekel" when Abraham purchases the cave of the Machpelah for his family's burial site. "And Abraham weighed to Ephron . . . four hundred shekels of silver, current money with the merchant" (Genesis 23:16).

In this context, however, we must remember that the shekel is a weight rather than a coin, since coins as we know them were not used over a wide area until after 600 B.C., well after the events of the Old Testament.

Even some later Biblical references to coins are anachronistic since they were written at a later time. Jews exiled in Babylonia no doubt saw silver sigloi and gold darics mentioned in the Bible. They were struck by Persian rulers beginning with Darius I (521–486 B.C.). Ironically these coins never circulated in ancient Israel. Probably the first coins to circulate there came from Athens, Macedon, Thasos and other Greek cities.

During the fifth century B.C., the Phoenician coastal cities of Sidon and Tyre began to strike silver coins, weighed by local shek-

Silver siglos of ancient Persia, showing the great king (Darius I) kneeling and shooting a bow.

Early shekel of Tyre, current money in the Holy Land for hundreds of years.

el standards, that became current in the Holy Land for hundreds of years. Shortly thereafter silver coins patterned after the Greek coins of Athens were issued in the Judean city of Gaza.

Some of these coins are of great interest, since they carry legends in ancient Aramaic referring to "YEHUD," the name of Judea, at the time a province of the great Persian Empire.

With the conquering of ancient Israel by Alexander the Great, a new mint at the city of Ake (today Akko) was established to produce large numbers of silver coins. After Alexander's death in 323 B.C., and the partition of his empire, the land of ancient Israel fell under the rule of the Seleucid kings of Syria.

Under the rule of Antiochus IV (175–164 B.C.), the Jews were severely persecuted and highly taxed. These abuses led to the revolt of Judah Maccabee and his brothers, who came from the town of Modiin in the Judean hills. This story is related in the books of the Maccabees.

Under the Maccabees, the Jews captured Jerusalem in 141 B.C. and became largely independent. One measure of this fact was that in 138 B.C., Antiochus VII specifically gave Simon Maccabee, the Jewish high priest, the right "to coin money for thy country with thine own stamp" (1 Maccabees 15:6).

It is known today that Simon Maccabee never was able to order the minting of coins for his nation, Antiochus VII apparently having withdrawn his goodwill. The coins previously believed to have been struck by Simon Maccabee, including the thick silver shekels, are now definitely dated to the period of the First Jewish War Against Rome. This dating was accomplished with the help of positive archaeological evidence.

Coin with the name Antiochus VII, anchor and lily, struck in Jerusalem 132–130 B.C.

There was one coin with the name of Antiochus VII and the date inscribed in Greek, struck in the years 132–130 B.C., that was probably struck in Jerusalem. On the obverse of this coin, instead of a portrait of Antiochus, there appears a lily, common emblem of Judea.

Today it is believed that the first coins struck independently by a Jewish king were issued by Alexander Jannaeus (103–76 B.C.), great nephew of Judah Maccabee. The coins of Jannaeus are probably the most common of the ancient Jewish coins. They carry designs of anchors, stars, cornucopias, flowers, and palm branches. These agricultural and maritime symbols appear frequently on the coins of the ancient Jews because of the Biblical edict against the use of "graven images."

Alexander Jannaeus.   *Alexander Jannaeus.*

Alexander Jannaeus.

However, a few of the later Jewish kings did allow their images to be struck upon coins.

Other Maccabean (or Hasmonean) kings who apparently issued coins were John Hyrcanus II (67 and 63–40 B.C.), Judah Aristobulus (67–63 B.C.), and Antigonus Mattathias (40–37 B.C.).

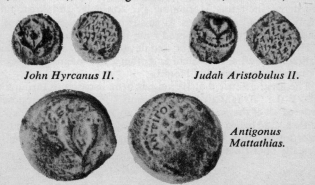

John Hyrcanus II.   *Judah Aristobulus II.*

Antigonus Mattathias.

Antigonus was the last of the Maccabean kings. Under his three-year rule of Judea he was almost constantly at war with Rome, since in 40 B.C. Herod the Great was made king by a declaration of the Roman senate and the approval of Augustus. One of the coins of Antigonus Mattathias depicts on the obverse the seven-branched menorah, or candelabra, used in the Temple services. The reverse of the coin has the image of the showbread table from the Temple.

In 37 B.C., with the help of the Roman general C. Sossius, Herod was finally able to besiege Jerusalem and capture it, along with Antigonus and his supporters. One of Herod's first official acts as king was to order death for forty-five members of the Sanhedrin, or Jewish high court.

Herod the Great.

Herod's rule of Judea was completely at the grace of Rome. The Romans made him "King of Judea," since he was not a member of a priestly family and therefore could not occupy the office of high priest, yet had to have a title equal or better in prestige.

Since Herod was not of a priestly family he sought to strengthen his ties with one, and so married Mariamme, a granddaughter of Hyrcanus II. Unfortunately for his family, however, Herod was paranoid about any potential threats to his power. Thus he eventually ordered a bloodbath in which a number of relatives were murdered, including Mariamme and Antipater and Aristobulus, his two sons by her. When Augustus heard of these murders he said, "It is better to be Herod's pig than his son."

Herod was a great builder, and developed the town of Sebaste-Samaria as well as Jerusalem and others. The magnificent second Temple was restored by Herod.

The great offense that Herod has been accused of through the ages is the "slaughter of the innocents," in which he supposedly ordered all of the male babies in the area of Bethlehem killed because he had heard that a future "king of the Jews" had been born, referring to Jesus. However, this "slaughter" has never been historically confirmed in any way.

Herod Archelaus

Herod Antipas

Herod Phillip II

Archelaus, Antipas, and Herod Philip II were the sons of Herod the Great, and they too issued coins.

Antipas was called "the fox" by Jesus, and he is mainly the Herod mentioned in the Bible. Antipas was the one who ordered the execution of John the Baptist, and it was to Antipas that Jesus was sent by the procurator Pontius Pilate.

Herod Agrippa I, grandson of Herod the Great, killed James and Peter (Acts 12:1–3). Other descendants of Herod who issued coins were Herod of Chalcis (brother of Agrippa I) and his son Aristobulus of Chalcis, and Agrippa II, son of Agrippa I.

Herod Agrippa I

Agrippa II

In 6 A.D. Judea was annexed to the Roman province of Syria, and the emperor Augustus appointed Coponius to the post of procurator—or governor—over Judea. He was the first of fourteen men to hold this position. With the exception of the three years Agrippa I reigned as king (41–44 A.D.) the procurators ruled until 66 A.D., when the First Jewish War Against Rome erupted. The procurators who issued coins were Coponius (6–9 A.D.), Marcus Ambibulus (9–12 A.D.), Valerius Gratus (15–26 A.D.), Pontius Pilate (26–36 A.D.), and Antonius Felix (52–54 A.D.).

Coponius   *M. Ambibulus*

Valerius Gratus   *Pontius Pilate*

Antonius Felix

Coins in the World of Jesus

There are a number of coins referred to in the New Testament, many of which are the types of coins that have been already described.

Tribute penny struck under Tiberius.

One of the most commonly cited coins mentioned in the New Testament is the "tribute penny." This coin is referred to in the story in which Jesus is asked, "Is it lawful to give tribute unto Caesar, or not?" (Matthew 22:17). This refers to the tax or tribute collected in the name of the emperor.

"Show me the tribute money. And they brought unto him a penny. And he saith unto them, Whose is this image and superscription? They say unto him, Caesar's. Then saith he unto them, Render therefore unto Caesar the things which are Caesar's; and unto God the things that are God's" (Matthew 22:19-21).

The particular coin referred to as the tribute penny is commonly thought to be the denarius (or silver penny) of Tiberius, which depicts Livia, his mother, on the reverse.

Another frequently discussed coin of the New Testament is the "widow's mite," or lepton. This is the coin referred to in the story from Mark (22:41-44).

      "Widow's mite."

"And Jesus sat over against the treasury, and beheld how the people cast money into the treasury: and many that were rich cast in much. And there came a certain poor widow, and she threw in two mites, which make a farthing. And he called unto him his disciples, and saith unto them, Verily I say unto you, That this poor widow hath cast more in, than all they which have cast into the treasury: For all they did cast in of their abundance; but she of her want did cast in all that she had . . . "

It is most commonly thought that these "mites" were the small bronze coins of the Maccabean kings. It is, however, also possible that the small coins of Herod the Great, Herod Archelaus, or even, perhaps, one of the early procurators could have been the widow's mite.

The final coin to which we will refer here is the silver shekel of Tyre, commonly thought to be the type of coin used to pay Judas for betraying Jesus. "And he [Judas] said unto them, What will ye give me, and I will deliver him [Jesus] unto you? And they covenanted with him for thirty pieces of silver" (Matthew 26:15).

These silver shekels and half-shekels of Tyre were also the coins accepted as the annual Temple tax. The priests arrived at the decision to accept these coins since they were of uniform good weight

    *Shekel of Tyre.*

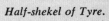 *Half-shekel of Tyre.*

and silver quality. Many people do not realize that the money changers who operated in the courts of the Temple served the purpose of converting Jewish bronze coins, or other bronze or silver coins, into the silver coins of Tyre so individuals could pay their annual Temple tax of 1 half-shekel.

The Jewish Revolts

The insults of the procurator Florus finally caused the uprising of the Jews against their Roman oppressors. Even though King Agrippa II warned that the Jews around the world would be "devastated by the enemy if you rebel," the war broke out. Initially the Jews routed the Roman garrisons stationed around Jerusalem—and indeed Jews in many cities were massacred in related incidents.

The famous thick silver shekels and half-shekels were struck for the five years of this war (66–70 A.D.). On the obverse the shekels show a chalice with a legend meaning "Shekel of Israel," and the date, and on the reverse they show three pomegranates on a stem surrounded by an inscription meaning "Jerusalem the Holy."

First Revolt shekel "Year 2."   *First Revolt shekel "Year 4."*

First Revolt half-shekel
"Year 1."

First Revolt half-shekel
"Year 3."

The Romans knew that the rebellion of this tiny nation had to be stamped out quickly lest other provinces of Rome get the wrong idea about Rome's strength.

*Small bronze coin of
the First Revolt.*

First Revolt bronze coin.

*First Revolt
bronze coin.*

Nero thus sent General Flavius Vespasian and his troops to Judea. Vespasian had led Rome's armies to victory in Germany and Britain. By the middle of 68, Vespasian and his men had succeeded in crushing the revolt in most of Judea. Only Jerusalem and the zealot fortress Massada remained. He prepared to take Jerusalem, but at about this time Nero died and civil wars rocked Rome. The Eastern legions proclaimed Vespasian emperor, and within the year he claimed the throne in Rome. He did not forget the Jews, however, and sent his son Titus to finish the job he had begun. Titus and his troops pounded the city and its walls, and besieged the city. Jerusalem's inhabitants were struck down by famine and plague as well as by enemy soldiers. In the year 70 the last wall fell, and the Temple burned. The golden Menorah and other holy implements of the Temple were taken to Rome and displayed. They have long since disappeared, but we are reminded of them by the reliefs on the arch that Titus had built in Rome to commemorate his victory over the tiny Jewish nation.

Sestertius of Vespasian "IVDAEA CAPTA."

Sestertius of Titus "IVD CAP."

Denarius of Vespasian showing a Jewess weeping beneath a victor's trophy, "IVDAEA."

Vespasian and Titus ordered a special series of coins to commemorate their victory. These coins carry legends such as "IVDAEA CAPTA," "IVDAEA DEVICTA," and simply "IVDAEA." The central device of virtually all of the Judaea Capta coins is a weeping Jewess; she usually sits mourning beneath a palm tree, the symbol of Judea. Some of the coins also show a victorious emperor, or sometimes Nike, dominating the scene wearing battle dress, with sword and spear, foot resting on a helmet.

Another fascinating Roman coin related to the Jews is a coin struck by the Emperor Nerva (96-98 A.D.). Under Domitian, Vespasian's other son, tax collectors vindictively attacked the Jews while collecting their money. One of their abuses was forcing a man to remove his clothes in public to see if he was circumcised and therefore a Jew. When Nerva became emperor, he let the tax remain, but abolished the rude method of collecting it. To proclaim his benevolence to the world, Nerva ordered a coin to be issued with a large palm tree and the inscription "FISCI IVDAICI CALVMNIA SVBLATA" ("The insult of the Jewish tax has been removed").

After the victory of Titus, Jews were expelled from Jerusalem, and Jewish communities developed around the ancient world. A number of Jews remained in Israel, and by 132 a new revolt of the Jews arose. The leader of this revolt was Simon Bar Kochba.

Sestertius struck by Nerva, commemorating "The Removal of the insult of the Jewish tax."

Bronze coins of Bar Kochba.

Silver coins of Bar Kochba.

Bar Kochba was a brilliant warrior in the tradition of Judah Maccabee. St. Jerome wrote that Bar Kochba gave the impression that he was "spewing out flames" when he rode into battle. He did this "by fanning a lighted blade of straw in his mouth with puffs of breath."

And when Bar Kochba's enemies hit him with their missiles, "he would catch the missiles from the enemy's catapults on one of his knees and hurl them back, killing many of the foe."

The coins of Bar Kochba are beautiful, with musical instruments, agricultural objects, palm trees, and wreaths. The silver tetradrachm depicts the facade of the second Temple, the only remaining visual record of that great edifice.

Many Jews and Romans were killed in the war, which ended in 135, when Hadrian renamed Jerusalem Aelia Capitolina, and banished Jews from the city.

(You can get a copy of my hardcover book Guide to Ancient Jewish Coins for $13.50 postpaid from Amphora, P.O. Box 630, West Haverstraw, NY 10993.)

Coins of Modern Israel

There would be no more coins struck by an independent Jewish nation for 1813 years, until 1948, when the State of Israel issued its first coins.

The trade coins of Israel are frequently patterned after the ancient coins. Israel's commemorative coins are also extremely pop-

Coins of modern Israel are designed with motifs of ancient coins of The Land.

ular with collectors around the world. Just how popular they are can be seen by the fact that the American Israel Numismatic Association is the second-largest organization of numismatists in the United States. The American Numismatic Association is the only group that is larger.

Modern Israeli coins can be ordered directly from the Israel Government Coins and Medals Corporation, 641 Lexington Ave., Sixth Floor, New York, NY 10022. They will put you on their free mailing list.

Many ancient Biblical coins as well as other ancient coins can be obtained from Amphora Coins, P.O. Box 630, West Haverstraw, NY 10993.

8. Mint Errors

Some beginning coin collectors simply can't understand why a person would want to specialize in collecting mistakes that another person—or a machine—has made.

Yet the collecting of numismatic errors is a fast-growing area of interest, and today there are many clubs, publications, and dealers specializing in studying and selling mint errors.

In a way it is ironic that this stage in coin collecting has been reached. Error collectors have arisen with the mechanization and near-perfection of the minting process. In Chapter 2 the basic steps involved in minting coins were explained. In ancient times there were no machine-tooled, well-oiled devices plunking out pressure-struck coins from flawless metal dies. Every die was engraved by hand. Every coin was struck by hand. Instead of the cleaner-than-clean rooms I have visited at mints in San Francisco or Birmingham, England, ancient mints more closely resembled primitive blacksmith shops—busier and noisier, though, than one you may have seen in Colonial Williamsburg.

Anyone who has looked at even a few ancient coins, whether Greek or Roman, can attest that what holds true for modern coins is *reversed* for the ancient series. That is, the vast majority of modern coins have been engraved and struck to perfection, but it is quite rare, to find an ancient coin that is perfect, or even near-perfect, in every respect. If the ancient coin is not a little off center, then it was struck on a broken planchet. If the planchet is perfect, then it has been double struck, or struck as a brockage. And so on.

So, as the minting process was perfected, and fewer mint mistakes were made, the error coins became increasingly rare. Today modern mint errors can bring thousands of dollars. But the misstruck ancient coins almost invariably bring only a fraction of the value of those coins that were struck perfectly. Thus the relative values of modern and ancient mint mistakes are proportionate to the relative rarity of the misstruck coins.

Many of the so-called "comprehensive" books about coin collecting have disparaged the entire field of collecting error coins.

These writers and supposed numismatic experts have failed to realize that many of the mint errors can be extremely valuable as educational items. The ancient misstruck coins, especially, can help us better understand the minting processes used in ancient times.

The fifth edition of the fine book *Modern Mint Mistakes* by Phillip Steiner and Michael Zimpfer divides modern mint errors into four major classifications:

- Denomination errors, which occur when a coin or a blank planchet is struck by dies not intended for that particular denomination
- Die errors, which occur when a mistake is made in the engraving or preparation of the dies. These errors are not one of a kind, but continue to repeat themselves until the die is removed from use
- Planchet errors, in which there is something wrong with the planchet before it was struck, and the error remains apparent even after the finished coin is produced
- Striking errors, which occur because of a mechanical malfunction by the presses that are used to strike the coins

Steiner and Zimpfer note that if the average person considers all of the various modern mint mistakes that are available, he may be misled into believing that the mints "specialize in mistakes."

The two experts quickly note, however, that "the opposite is true. The one thing each mint would like to see discontinued altogether is errors. But with high speed production and numerous deadlines to meet, a few mistakes are bound to occur; most of them are caught in screening mechanisms. The majority of these errors is due to mechanical malfunctions, with only a small fraction accounted to human error."

Among error collectors the saying is that the rarest errors are the ones that never get out of the mint.

In spite of that statement, however, one cannot rule out the possibility that many of the more unusual mint errors have been deliberately created by mint employees and then smuggled out of the mint facility. This is more likely to have been done years ago, when the United States mint was not as mechanized, and security was not as strict as it is today. Occasionally one will hear or read a story about just this kind of situation, and how a mint employee has illegally smuggled out a weird variety of a coin in some imaginative way.

The novice collector of error coins must beware of forged errors. It is far easier for the swindler to attempt to forge a mint error than an actual coin, because to forge a rare coin one must start from the very beginning of the entire minting process, but in the case of numismatic errors, one can simply take a coin from circulation and try to mutilate it in a way that mimics a genuine mint error. Fortunately, even the most sophisticated error forgers cannot duplicate all of the subtleties of genuine mint errors, and thus experts in this field can authoritatively identify error coins.

Here is a rundown of some of the commonly available mint errors in the four classifications mentioned earlier.

Denomination Errors

Incorrect planchet errors occur when coins are struck upon a planchet of the same metal but meant for a different denomination. Thus one could have a dollar struck on the planchet for a fifty-cent piece (abbreviated as $1/50¢), a dollar struck on a planchet meant for a quarter ($1/25¢), a dollar struck on a planchet meant for a dime ($1/10¢), a half-dollar struck on a quarter plan-

1852 large cent struck on half-cent planchet.

chet (50¢/25¢), a half-dollar struck on a dime planchet (50¢/10¢), and a quarter struck on a dime planchet (25¢/10¢). It is extremely rare to find a coin struck upon a planchet meant for a *larger* coin. The value of this and other errors is enhanced considerably when the date of the coin is visible, and the most desirable are when the largest denomination is struck on the smallest planchet.

Incorrect metal errors occur when coins are struck on a planchet made of a different metal, and meant for a different-denomination coin. Thus we may find a half-dollar meant to be struck on a silver or clad planchet struck, instead, on the planchet for a nickel (50¢/5¢). It's also possible to have the dollar, half-dollar, quarter, or dime struck upon planchets made for nickels or cents, etc. In this category, too, it is very rare to find a coin struck on a planchet meant for a larger coin.

Transition errors are really just a continuation of the wrong-metal or incorrect-planchet errors. They occur when the mint changes the metal upon which a particular coin is struck, but some coins are accidentally struck on the previous metal. For example, the 1943 cents were struck in zinc, but a very few were struck on copper planchets. Likewise, in 1944, when the mint reverted to copper cents, a very few were struck in steel. There are also 1942 and 1946 silver nickels, even though the official wartime silver nickels were struck in 1943, 1944, and 1945. There are some rare examples of 1964 clad coinage (which did not officially begin until 1965) and some 1965 coins struck in silver instead of on the official clad alloy.

Double denomination errors are another logical progression in the various denomination errors. These occur when a coin of a different denomination is accidentally struck on a coin that has already been struck, such as a half-dollar being struck upon a cent, or a dollar being struck upon a quarter.

Since the United States mint is sometimes commissioned by foreign countries to manufacture their coins, it is also possible for a United States coin to be struck upon a foreign coin, or vice versa. In the last ten or so years, United States mints have made coins for Brazil, Canada, Costa Rica, the Dominican Republic, Ethiopia, Israel, Korea, Mexico, and the Philippines, among other nations. Thus there have been, for example, U.S. quarters struck on 1 cent-stukken of the Netherlands East Indies, U.S. cents struck on Costa Rican 5 centimos, U.S. nickels struck on Panamanian 1/10 balboas, and so on.

Die Errors

Broken, chipped, or cracked dies cause many of the commonly found error specimens today. Even though the dies that are used to strike coins today are precision instruments made under careful quality control, they can become damaged because of the wear and tear of lengthy use. Sometimes, of course, there are weaknesses in a particular piece of metal, and sometimes machinery malfunctions cause dies to crack or break.

Among the common and popular types of these errors are the *BIE* and *LIBERTY* errors. These occur when the portion of the 1-cent die in which the word "*LIBERTY*" is written chips slightly, and makes it appear as if the word is misspelled. Some of the varieties include cents in which the word appears to be spelled LIBIERTY, LIIBERTY, LIBEIRTY, LIBERITY, ILIBIERTY, LIIBIERTY, and LIBERTIY.

When a die is severely cracked it can show as a ridge across the surface of a coin, caused when the planchet metal is forced into the die crack.

Another kind of die break is a *cud*, which results when a small piece of metal of the die breaks away. This results in what appears to be a small, raised blob of metal on the coin surface. If the cud or break is large enough, it may cause so much metal from the planchet to flow into it that corresponding areas of other parts of the coin will be very weakly struck or not struck at all.

Clashed die errors occur when for some reason a blank planchet is not fed into the coin press and the two dies clash against each other with their fifty or so tons of striking pressure instead of against the planchet. The resultant damage the dies inflict upon each other is then passed along to subsequent coins they strike. A coin that has been struck from such damaged dies will have incused portions of the obverse design on the reverse, and vice versa.

Other damage can also occur to the dies. Sometimes tools or other objects may fall on the dies, or the dies will be scratched as they are polished. When these accidents occur, of course, any damage to the dies will be passed directly along to the coins that are struck from them. Sometimes mint workers try to heavily polish dies to remove scratches, gouges, clashmarks, dirt, or grease. In doing so, they may wear down the metal of the die, and the coins struck from such an overly polished die will not have as much detail as normal. It takes a good bit of study to tell the difference between a coin struck from an overly polished die and a coin that has simply been worn down in circulation. The best way to tell the difference, of course, is to examine only uncirculated coins in seeking this minor error.

Filled dies cause another related type of misstruck coin. A filled die can occur when dirt, grease, or bits of metal fill up a portion of a die and cause blank or very weak areas in the coin.

Mint mark errors are especially interesting. Many collectors don't realize that mint marks aren't engraved into the dies with the rest of the design. Instead the mint marks are struck onto the dies with a hand-held punch. If it takes more than a single strike with the engraver's hammer, a double image of the mint mark may occur. In rare instances, one mint mark has been punched right upon a different one. This error caused, for example, the 1938 and 1955 D/S nickels as well as the rare 1944 S/D cent, among others.

Double die errors occur when the die is made. Sometimes there is an improper alignment between the time the first and second impressions are made on the die from the hub. This slight misalignment can cause a doubling error in which a doubled image is created. The most famous example of this is the 1955 doubled-die cent, which has brought more than $500.

Engraving errors occur when a mistake is made in engraving the die. In the early years of the mint, since there was no mass-production method of making dies, they were often re-engraved to lengthen their life. The popular small and large mint mark variations are also included in this classification.

Overdates are caused when two different hubs are used to create a single working die. Thus the 1942/1 dime and the 1918/17 quarter were struck.

Rotated dies are still another kind of die error. If you hold a United States coin by the edges between your thumb and forefinger (thumb at bottom, forefinger on top) and swivel the coin from obverse to reverse, you will see that they are aligned at a 180° difference. That is, if you rotate a coin in this way, the obverse will be right side up, and the reverse upside down. This is the way United States coins are meant to be struck. Occasionally, however, the dies become loose and rotate relative to each other. Such errors are measured according to the number of degrees the dies have rotated. Thus if a die has rotated 180 degrees, it will strike a coin with both obverse and reverse facing in the same direction when rotated between thumb and forefinger as described above. When specifying rotation, be sure to note whether the movement has been clockwise or counterclockwise. Variances up to 5° are common, and those of more than 30° are considered to be scarce.

Planchet Errors

Damaged-planchet errors occur when a coin is struck upon a defective planchet. The most commonly occurring of these defective planchets are called *clips*, which are really incomplete planchets. They occur when the planchets are being punched out of strips of metal. Sometimes the punch overlaps on a hole already punched out, and a curved clip results. Straight clips can occur when planchets are punched too close to the end of a strip of metal. Unusual and popular bowtie clips are, in fact, not planchets at all, but are the scrap metal from between planchets. One might think it would be simple to take a coin and whack off a portion of it, thus producing what would appear to be a clip. However, there is a phenomenon known as the Blakesley effect, which occurs in most (but not all) genuine clips. The result of this effect is a slight bulge on the coin's rim opposite the clip. An expert can also observe the metal flow that has occurred when authenticating a clipped planchet.

Fragment errors occur when small fragments of metal happen to fall between two dies. These tiny pieces must be less than a quarter of the normal weight of the coin in order to qualify as fragments, and must also be struck on both sides, and thinner than normal.

Metal irregularities in the planchet can cause errors. Sometimes there are errors made in preparing the metal. If the alloy is not uniform in consistency, streaks of various metals can occur throughout coins. If the coins are not treated properly during processing, other minor errors in tone or surface can also occur. When impurities become trapped inside the molten metal when it is cooling, other irregularities can occur. A common one is the *lamination*, in which a part of the surface metal of the coin actually begins to peel or flake away.

Other unusual planchet errors can occur. Sometimes, for example, the planchets may have been punched from stock too thick or too thin. Thus there exist quarters struck on planchets made from half-dollar stock, half-dollars struck on quarter stock, quarters struck on dime stock, and dollars struck on half-dollar stock, as well as other variations.

Freak errors occur when a washer accidentally falls into a hopper of planchets, or a press, and becomes struck. These *washer coins* are extremely rare and valuable.

Striking Errors

One of the most obvious striking (or nonstriking) errors is when a planchet is not struck at all, resulting in a *blank planchet.* Another obvious one is the *double strike* or *multiple strike*, in which the coin receives a second, third, or more impressions from the dies. A flipover double strike occurs when the coin flips over in the dies before it is restruck, and thus has obverse and reverse on one side and obverse and reverse on the other.

*Blank planchet
for half-dime.*

*1863 Indian Head cent
triple struck.*

1795 Silver Dollar double struck.

1922 Silver Dollar struck without collar.

Off-center errors occur when a coin does not get placed fully between the dies, and is struck only partially. Usually the more off-center the coin has been struck, the more valuable it will be.

Folded-over errors occur when a coin somehow lands in between the dies on edge, the dies strike together, and their tremendous pressure causes the coin to fold in half while being struck. If the coin is not folded over, but is actually struck on its edges, an error called an *edge strike* occurs.

Broadstruck coins occur when the collar that usually surrounds the planchet while it is being struck does not come into place properly, and the coin spreads out too much while it is being struck.

Brockages occur when a part of the coin is struck in incuse. This most frequently occurs when a coin that has been struck sticks to the reverse die and another planchet enters between the dies. This

1863 Civil War token brockage.

second planchet is struck by the obverse die on one side, and by the other struck coin, now called a cap (because it caps the die), on the reverse side. Since the surface of the cap which will strike the planchet has a normal image of the portrait (as opposed to the negative image of the die), it will impress the incused or negative image of the portrait. This error rarely occurs on the reverse of the coin since it is not as likely that a coin will stick in the obverse die (the reverse design thus becoming the cap), since it is always moving up and down. The *cap* itself becomes another error, since the continued pressure of striking coins can cause it to become saucer-shaped, and distorted on at least one side.

Impressed errors occur when some foreign material—such as a staple, wire, string, or piece of cloth—becomes imbedded in the surface of the coin while it is being struck. These are not all that uncommon, since a large number of foreign materials are used in the mints, to clean and maintain the presses and other machinery. Thus fragments are frequently struck into the surfaces of coins in this way.

9. How to Grade Coins

In years past the grading of coins was not very significant. But with the advent of investment collecting and the tremendous volume of mail-order coin buying, many coin dealers and collectors today will tell you flatly that grading is the key to all knowledge as far as coin collecting is concerned.

This is mainly true. Once most coin transactions were on a face-to-face basis. There was no need to grade coins because the seller could see what he was selling at the same time the buyer saw what he was buying. If the buyer didn't like the looks of the coin relative to the price, he simply said no to the deal.

As the number of coin collectors increased in recent years, the problem of describing coins became more important. Today literally hundreds of coin transactions take place through the mails every day. And the price structure of most coins is such that the price difference between grades—especially the better grades—is of major significance. Thus if a collector buys a coin that is Extra Fine, but is led to believe that the coin is actually Bright Uncirculated, the coin will be worth substantially less than the collector thinks. (On the other hand, the shrewd collector may occasionally find a coin that has been *undergraded*, which he can buy for substantially less than the market price. This rarely occurs, however, since the tendency is often to *overgrade*. In fact, "steal" prices are a good warning signal that coins are heavily overgraded.)

Some unscrupulous dealers take advantage of a process known as "whizzing," which is a kind of buffing, to make coins look as if they are higher in grade than they actually are. This occurs because the whizzing buffs the metal and covers points of wear. All cleaned coins are not considered to have been whizzed. Various methods of coin cleaning are discussed in Chapter 11.

It is not difficult to understand why a collector who does not understand coin grading can get into trouble.

Fortunately most coin dealers will carefully and honestly grade the coins they sell. But some dealers are downright dishonest when it comes to grading coins; they will deliberately overgrade coins, price them as if they were very cheap for grade, and sell them to unsuspecting collectors.

Luckily, the entire responsible numismatic fraternity—including national and local organizations, reputable dealers, and major publications such as *Coin World*—has made it a point to crusade against these dishonest dealers whenever possible. The better numismatic publications try very hard to eliminate advertisers when they are known to overgrade or otherwise cheat their customers. Collectors should always beware of the possibility of overgrading, since lapses can occur. Even the most reputable dealer will occasionally grade a coin incorrectly. This is no surprise considering the number of coins that the average dealer works with in a given period of time. Such dealers, of course, will quickly exchange the coin in question for one that is properly graded, or issue an immediate cash refund for it. We feel that when a dealer has inadvertently sold an overgraded coin to a customer, the dealer should not only be responsible for making an immediate refund, but should also pay any postage costs the customer has incurred in making the purchase.

A Study in Overgrading

Donn Pearlman, a coin collector who is also a radio newsman for WBBM, the CBS Radio affiliate in Chicago, undertook a three-month investigation of coin dealers from mid-January to mid-April 1977. His investigation was assisted by several Chicago coin dealers, the local Better Business Bureau, and Virgil Hancock, then president of the American Numismatic Association. Pearlman reported on his investigation in the July 1977 issue of *The Numismatist*, official monthly magazine of the ANA.

Over a period of three months a definite pattern was established for four mail-order firms. Evidence was later received for a fifth. While 11 of the 16 firms we received orders from sent coins as advertised, five rather consistently shipped overgraded merchandise.

A total of 47 coins were ordered ranging in retail price from $9 to $349.50 each. In two cases we could show an apparent pattern of the dealer buying coins in EF/AU condition and advertising to sell those same types of coins in Choice and Gem BU, usually at below prevailing wholesale prices for such items. It was enough to arouse a few suspicions.

Example: One dealer advertised on a teletype circuit to

purchase slider [numismatic slang which means "sliding" between two grades] 1932-D quarters for $165.00 each. A month later he impressively advertised in a coin publication to sell Choice BU 1932-D quarters for $349.50 each, about $200 below what most dealers would pay for such an item. The two separate 1932-D pieces we received from that dealer were each judged to be only XF/AU.

This is just one unfortunate example of what we have been talking about.

To protect yourself from buying coins that are overgraded you should make it a point to obtain at least one of three key books that carefully illustrate grading on major types of United States coins. They are:

- *A Guide to the Grading of United States Coins* by M.R. Brown and J.W. Dunn
- *Photograde—A Photographic Grading Guide for U.S. Coins* by J.F. Ruddy
- *Official ANA Grading Standards* published by the Whitman Publishing Company.

What the Grades Mean

In its 1967 publication *Introduction to Numismatics: A Symposium*, the American Numismatic Association published an elementary list of the meanings of the various coin grades. Here are those definitions:

Uncirculated (Unc.)—in perfect condition showing no signs of wear or damage but not necessarily brilliant; Sometimes known as Mint State

Extremely Fine (EF,XF)—no definite signs of wear but having a less desirable surface than an uncirculated coin

Very Fine (VF)—showing inconsequential signs of wear but only slightly less desirable than the preceding classification

Fine (F)—perceptible signs of wear but still a desirable piece

Very Good (VG)—definite signs of wear but not altogether unattractive

Good (G)—worn but lettering and design all clear

Fair (FR)—quite badly worn and usually undesirable

Poor (P)—less desirable than Fair, yet the design can usually be distinguished

Lincoln Cents in Varying Conditions

Uncirculated   Extremely Fine

Very Fine   Fine

Very Good   Good

Fair   Poor

It is simple to see why we recommend that you obtain one of the books devoted to discussions of grading coins. Grading is something of a relative and subjective operation unless some rather basic ground rules are understood and accepted. Only by looking at detailed and enlarged photographs or drawings will you be able to learn to grade coins properly.

When a dealer describes coins on a list or catalogue, he will also list any defects in the coin such as nicks, scratches, or other markings. The color of a coin is also important, since with time coins will often acquire a natural toning. Some collectors find this toning desirable, others do not.

Sheldon's Grading System

In his book *Penny Whimsy*, Dr. William H. Sheldon describes a quantitative scale grading system in an attempt to establish a firm basis for grading coins. Here are Sheldon's grading numbers:

1	Poor
2	Fair
3	About Good
4-6	Good
8-10	Very Good
12-15	Fine
20-25-30-35	Very Fine
40-45	Extremely Fine
50-55	About Uncirculated
60-65-70	Uncirculated

Sheldon's system is such that a coin in Very Fine condition, for example, could be listed in several ways. If it barely qualified as a Very Fine coin it would be a VF-20, but if it was the best possible Very Fine, but didn't quite make Extremely Fine, it would be called a VF-35. The VF-25 and VF-30 would fall somewhere in between those extremes. Sheldon's system is quite a precise one, and has been widely adopted by many dealers.

Here is a more detailed description of the way Sheldon listed his grading numbers in *Penny Whimsy*. It may seem complicated, but ask any friendly and reliable dealer to take a few moments to explain this system to you, since it is becoming increasingly popular.

1	Basal State	The coin is not mutilated, and can be identified, but it is so badly worn that only part of the design is visible. Type must be identified, but date may be worn away in certain cases.
2	Fair	At least half of the inscription and the design, as well as the date, can be seen.
3	Very Fair	The date and most of the detail can be seen, but the coin may still be nearly worn smooth.
4	Good	The date and all of the detail are clear, but it is still very worn.
5		

6		
7	Very Good	Entire design and inscription of coin are very clear, but coin shows uniform signs of wear on all portions.
8		
10		
12	Fine	Complete design and all inscriptions are sharp. Heavy wear on high points. Under magnification, there is no microscopic detail.
15		
20	Very Fine	Complete design, inscriptions, etc., are in sharp relief. Wear shows only on highest points, even under magnification. Microscopic details remain except on high points.
30		
40	Extremely Fine	High points show only very slight traces of wear.
50	About Uncirculated	Good magnification is needed to show that the coin is not perfect.
60	Mint State	Coin shows no signs of wear. Writes Sheldon: "For condition 60 a minor blemish, perhaps some microscopic injury, or light trace of discoloration may be tolerated. For condition 70, the coin must be exactly as it left the dies. . . . Condition 60 means Mint State. Condition 70 means *perfect* Mint state."

Grading Ancient Coins

While grading all modern coins is essentially the same, the grading standards will change slightly with regard to ancient coins. This is logical, since even the most perfect coin that has been laying in the ground for 2,000 years would be unlikely to match a modern BU coin.

Also, the method of grading modern coins was designed to describe machine-made coins. The ancient coins, however, as we described earlier, are all handmade. They may be struck a little too hard, or a little too light. Flan cracks, rough edges, porous surfaces, heavy scratches, and poor centering are only a few of the factors that must be taken into consideration. To date no perfect method of grading ancient coins has been developed. In his book *The Illustrated Grading Guide to Ancient Numismatics* (JSD Publications), Raymond Ladd has given us a starting point for developing a more standardized method of grading ancient coins.

Writes Ladd: "One approaches grading, in ancient numismatics, by first passing fair judgment on the overall appearance of the coin surface. That is to say, how the coin held up under the care of minting and the wear of circulation. The second rule, in grade formulation, is to take into consideration, or add to the proposed grade, the minor to major desecrations that may have taken their toll on the coin planchet over the last two hundred decades."

Here are Ladd's grade definitions for ancient coins:

FDC—The Fleur de Coin is that rare, perfect jewel of the mint master's art which is characterized by complete, sharply struck detail and nearly perfect centering, with a full border (where one exists), on a full round flan (unless the coin was designed otherwise). The slightest hint of wear, nicks, corrosion or any other defects will disqualify a coin from attaining this grade. Ancient coins, in FDC, average no more than two to three coins per hundred thousand sold.

Extremely Fine—A coin, in Extremely Fine condition, is characterized by a good round flan, little or no wear, except on the very highest detail, good centering and no objectionable corrosion. All details should be clearly defined with at least ninety percent of the existing inscription legible. Minor nicks, flan and die cracks may be expected in this grade as well.

Very Fine—A coin, in Very Fine condition, is characterized by noticeable wear on the high detail. Good centering is still desirable, with at least seventy-five percent of the existing inscription legible. One may also expect an increase in the volume of cracks, scratches, corrosive pitting and other planchet defects, as well as a noticeable reduction in the normal coin weight.

Fine—A coin, in Fine condition, is characterized by considerable wear, on the lower detail, in addition to an increase in the volume of cuts, scratches, medium to heavy corrosion and other planchet defects. A loss of up to fifty percent of the existing inscription and twenty percent of the design is not uncommon in this grade. A reduction in normal coin weight will be considerable in this grade as well.

Very Good—Very Good is the lowest grade type commonly found in collections. It is usually a filler grade, greatly worn, and suffering from an intensely high percentage of planchet defects. A loss of more than sixty percent of the existing inscription is not uncommon in this grade.

Good—Coins, in Good condition, are characterized by monumental wear and subject to the full range of planchet defects common, or uncommon, to ancient coinage. A loss of more than seventy percent of the existing inscription and design is not uncommon. Coins in this grade are, often as not, uniface and are rendered into collections as a last resort, in reverence to the coin's great rarity or out of respect to the lack of purchasing power on the part of the collector.

Ladd makes a noteworthy remark about so-called Mint State ancient coins:

"Fleur de Coin and Mint State, while synonymous terms in modern coinage, too often have quite a different meaning in ancient numismatics. We feel that a certain clarification and even division of these terms must be made here. It is often to the collector's dismay and great dissatisfaction that, while using the term 'mint state,' in describing a coin's condition as being as perfect as the day it was struck, the seller may unwisely fail to add the fact that the coin may also be double struck, flat struck or struck on worn or corroded dies, etc. Coins in Mint condition can range in grade from Extremely Fine to Good and a coin, if not a true FDC, should be qualified as to its actual condition by a description of any defects that may have occurred during minting."

Buying Coins Abroad

If you are a collector of world coins or ancient coins you will probably at one time buy coins from a foreign dealer either via a fixed price list or an auction catalogue. To help you understand how a particular coin is being graded, we offer the following list of United States grades and translations of those grades into German and French, two languages which you will most probably encounter besides English. It is worth mentioning that in Europe ancient coins especially are graded on a somewhat more conservative basis, and this is worth keeping in mind when reading European price lists.

English	German	French
Uncirculated	Stempelglanz	Fleur de Coin
Extremely Fine	Vorzüglich	Superbe
Very Fine	Sehr Schön	Très Beau
Fine	Schön	Beau
Very Good	Sehr Gut Erhalten	Très Bien Conservé
Good	Gut Erhalten	Bien Conservé
Fair	Schlecht Erhalten	Mal Conservé

10. Cataloguing and Photographing Your Coins

Maintaining a large coin collection can be a time-consuming pastime, especially if the collection is constantly being changed by adding and trading off duplicates and upgrading the conditions of the coins.

It is advisable to keep careful records of all the coins in your collection, including photographs and other descriptive material. This will protect you in case of theft or fire, or in case your heirs unexpectedly find themselves with a coin collection as part of your estate.

Cataloguing

For my own collection I have adapted a rather simple, but complete, filing system. Each coin acquired is numbered consecutively and entered into a logbook with the date of acquisition, price, type, and place purchased.

Then an index card, adapted from cards used by the Israel Museum in Jerusalem, is completed. Each 3×5 inch index card contains spaces for the following information:

    1. Number of the coin in my collection (the same number as entered in the logbook described above)
    2. Period of the coin's issue, or ruler under whom the coin was issued
    3. Material from which the coin was made
    4. Mint at which the coin was struck
    5. Denomination of the coin
    6. Diameter of the coin
    7. Weight of the coin
    8. Rarity of the coin, if significant
    9. Description of the coin's obverse
    10. Photograph of the coin's obverse
    11. Description of the coin's reverse

12. Photograph of the coin's reverse
13. Bibliography or other reference number of coin type
14. Coded price and time of purchase of coin

These cards, complete with black-and-white photographs of the coins, are kept in metal file boxes which are always available at home. This is a significant factor, since the valuable coin collection should never be kept at home as a security precaution. Yet many collectors want to study their collection frequently without removing the coins from the bank safety deposit box. Thus these photo-file cards are an excellent solution.

Plaster Casts of Coins

Another good solution, if you are a collector of old or ancient coins (but not modern or proof coins), is making plaster casts of your coins.

A plaster cast is an almost exact replica of each side of your coin. It has the same relief, along with all of the flaws. Many of the famous coin books show photographs only of plaster casts, and not of the coins themselves. One good reason for this is that ancient coins often contain certain discolorations that distract from the actual relief of the coin. When the coin's exact image is transferred to a plaster cast, it becomes quite an easy matter to photograph the piece without such distractions.

Here's my method of making plaster casts.

MAKING THE MOLD

1. Use an oil-base modeling clay (plasticine), such as that used by florists in arranging flowers, or that used by children in modeling.
2. Knead a piece of the clay until it is workable, then roll it into a sphere the size of a golf ball. Place the ball on a smooth, clean, flat surface and squash it slightly with the palm of your hand. Peel up and turn it over and you will have a smooth, flat surface of clay.
3. Powder this surface lightly with baby or talcum powder. This will keep the coin from sticking to the clay.
4. Press the coin evenly into the ball, to at least half of the coin's thickness.
5. Turn the mold over and shake it slightly to make the coin fall out. (Don't let the coin drop and get damaged.)
6. The mold is now ready to use.

MIXING THE PLASTER

1. Use a fine grade of dental plaster of Paris. It should have a drying time of at least 20 minutes.

2. If you want to color the plaster slightly, add a tiny bit of paint powder. Earthen colors are most effective.

3. Make a thin mix of the plaster, about the consistency of whipping cream. The proportion should be about two teaspoons of *cold* water to a generous tablespoon of plaster. You may need to experiment a bit to get the best mix. Don't mix too much plaster at one time.

MAKING THE CAST

1. First use a small, fine paint brush and apply plaster to the inside of the mold. Don't press too hard on the brush, but sweep it gently into all of the nooks and corners of the mold.

2. Tap the bottom of the mold sharply against the top of the table to cause any bubbles in the plaster thus far applied to rise and burst. Practice will give you the feel of this technique and you will be able to tap the mold on the table without distorting it at all.

3. Fill the mold with plaster.

4. Tap it another couple of times against the table top to dislodge any more bubbles.

5. After about 45 minutes remove the cast from the mold by gently pushing aside the edges of the mold. The plaster cast will fall right into your hands.

6. With a penknife or other tool trim the edges of the mold, and flatten the back of it.

7. Allow it to dry completely for 12 to 24 hours, then, if desired, mount it on an index card with white glue.

8. If the mold has not been ruined it can be used again. The clay, however, should probably be discarded instead of used for another coin, since tiny bits of plaster may cling to it and will ruin other casts.

Photographing Your Coins

"The most difficult things to photograph are those that are farthest away or closest," says George Gilbert, who is both a coin collector and a photographic expert.

He explains that a large number of coin collectors are frustrated in their attempts to photograph their coins because they "try to use cameras designed for six to eight feet at the beach to work at six to eight inches. They try to force the camera to work for something that it wasn't designed for."

We *have* seen coin collectors who have taken pictures of their coins using fixed-focus snapshot cameras. But the pictures aren't very good.

For good-quality coin photographs, here are a few tips:

1. Use a camera with changeable lenses.
2. Use a single lens reflex camera so the image you see is the same one you are photographing.
3. To get close to the coin you can use either a zoom closeup attachment for your normal lens, a specially designed macro lens, or extension tubes or bellows which will, in essence, convert your normal lens to a closeup lens.
4. Use a copy stand or tripod on which to mount your camera.
5. Use a cable release to minimize vibrations.
6. Shoot at the smallest possible f-stop to maximize depth of field and sharpness.
7. If you shoot outside in the daylight do it before ten A.M. or after three P.M. so the light will come in on the coin from an angle. Use a small white card or a pocket mirror to reflect light back onto the coin for maximum contrast and detail, and minimum shadow.
8. When shooting indoors with artificial light, be sure to use indoor film if you are shooting in color.
9. Indoors you will have to adjust the light source to suit the coin's relief and finish. Coins with a high shine may give off considerable glare. Ask your photographic supplier to tell you about polarizing filters if this proves to be a problem. A simple trick to help eliminate glare is to cover the artificial light sources with white pocket handkerchiefs while photographing such coins.
10. Place the light at an angle with coins of high relief, to maximize detail and contrast. If the coin is of low relief, as are most modern coins, you can try putting the light source directly above the coin. With a tiny ball of paper placed under one edge of the coin, tilt it so it reflects the light right back into the lens of the camera. Don't use too big a ball of paper or the coins will seem to be oval instead of round!
11. Use a background that contrasts with your coin, if you

like, but do not use a background with a strong pattern that will detract from the coin. I prefer to use a plain white background.

12. Place the coin on a small plastic block or sugar cube to separate it from the background.

13. If you are using color film, use the fastest-speed film possible. With black-and-white film, use Plus-X or its equivalent. Only use the slow, fine-grained black-and-white films such as Panatomic-X if you are going to enlarge the photograph tremendously.

14. Make sure that your camera is level with the ground. You can do this by placing a small spirit level on the camera back and keeping your eye on the air bubble to make sure it stays centered.

If you expect to do a lot of coin photography you may want to inquire among several coin dealers to see what kind of special coin-photography setups are currently available. There are, for example, special mounts for Polaroid-type cameras, complete with fixed-focal-length lens, special mounting, and built-in light.

11. Cleaning Coins

At one time or another you are going to want to know about cleaning coins. There is little help in the advice that many books, many collectors, and many dealers will give: "Don't clean your coins."

Most of the time that *is* good advice. Very good advice! But the most important question is not whether to clean or not to clean, but when a coin does need cleaning.

Modern foreign coins and United States coins very rarely need to be cleaned. If you do try to clean any of these coins, and are not an expert at it, you stand a very good chance of reducing the coin's value to near zero.

For some reason a certain number of collectors feel that they want to have all of their modern coins looking as if they have just fallen from the dies. That is a very nice wish, but it is rather impractical, since, as we all know, metals such as bronze and silver will tarnish over the years. This tarnish, when it occurs on coins, is called "toning."

We believe that there is nothing more attractive than a nicely kept modern bronze or silver coin that has acquired a lovely dark, iridescent tone. The tone is caused by the reaction of the coin's surface with the air and the chemicals suspended in it. You would be wise, of course, to protect your coins from the ravages of severe air pollution. But some contact with the air is inevitable, and thus coins will invariably tone over a period of years.

You should be warned, however, that coin trays and coin holders, if they are not made properly, can also contain harsh chemicals that can cause your coins to rapidly tarnish, or even begin to corrode. Water, especially seawater, can also have this effect.

The only way I know to positively inhibit toning is to coat your coins with a thin layer of lacquer as soon as you obtain them. If this process is properly done—and you should check with your coin dealer for information on the best material to use—it is not objectionable to most numismatists. There is the chance, however, that lacquered coins may bring less than unlacquered coins when they are sold.

There are certain occasions when you will have good cause to have a modern coin cleaned. Several years ago, for example, I found an old scrapbook in the basement of my parent's home. A silver dollar had been taped into it—it was a silver dollar I had received as a birthday gift on my first birthday. The coin was not a particularly rare one, but I decided to put it in my collection. Unfortunately, over more than two decades the cellophane tape had become yellow and brittle, and stuck tight to the coin.

It is also possible that you may find an old coin that has become encrusted with dirt over the decades, and you'll want to clean it up a bit so you can identify it. As a first measure you can try mild soap and water, which will remove any surface dirt.

One trick in cleaning coins is to *clean, but never overclean*. There is no reason that a circulated Indian Head cent from 1898 should look as shiny as a brass belt buckle. Nobody would expect an 80-year-old circulated cent to look new, especially an experienced dealer or collector.

Q. David Bowers, a well-known coin dealer, observes, "Cleaning any coin that grades less than About Uncirculated in condition will generally produce an unnatural appearance that is not acceptable to most collectors. The cleaning of *copper* coins in any grade should be avoided unless it is absolutely necessary to remove an unsightly fingerprint or large carbon or corrosion spot."

Before I tell you how to clean coins, let me remind you that you should *not try to clean coins that do not need cleaning*. Some of you will no doubt be tempted to clean *all* of the coins in your collection so they will all have a similar finish. Don't do it! This will give your collection a very artificial look, and will no doubt *decrease its value*. Remember: Cleaning coins is not strictly taboo, but more coins have been harmed by cleaning than have been helped.

The best way to clean a modern silver or bronze coin that *needs cleaning* is with one of the commercially available clear liquid coin dips. *Do not* use powders, pastes, or polishes. Rubbing a coin while cleaning it will certainly cause it far more harm than good. *Carefully* follow the directions on the dip container. It is always a good idea to try it a few times on coins that are not worth anything to you. In this way you will get a feel for the dipping process, and perfect your method before taking a chance with one of your valuable coins.

After dipping you must immediately rinse the coin in cool, running water. Make sure all chemicals are completely removed (but no rubbing). Now pat your coin dry with a soft, clean, absorbent cloth.

It is very important that your coins be completely dry before you store them. Make sure that your hands are also clean and dry when putting coins away, because even a little moisture in a closed envelope can ruin a valuable coin in a very short time.

Coin Care is a good product available at most coin dealers. It will help you remove light layers of dirt, oxidation, or grease from copper coins.

If you find a silver dollar with old tape stuck on it, as I did, or if you want to remove bits of glue or paint from a coin's surface, your best bet is the solvent acetone. Don't rub and scrub. Just let the coin soak in a bit of acetone for a few minutes, then remove it, rinse with water and pat dry. If some of the material remains, repeat the process.

Never use acetone or any other solvent in a closed room or near a flame. Such chemicals can cause inhalation poisoning, or fires.

If you find an old silver coin with green oxide on it, and the only way to salvage the coin is by cleaning it, try a soak in household ammonia. The ammonia may dissolve away the corrosion, and then you can rinse and carefully dry the coin.

Cleaning Ancient Coins

Unlike modern coins, a very large number of ancient coins *must* be cleaned. Since these coins lie in the ground for hundreds or even thousands of years before they are found, they often acquire a thick layer of encrustation which sometimes must be removed before the coin can even be identified.

It is not easy to remove such an encrustation safely from ancient coins, and this is a job for experts. There are some types of oxidation that are extremely desirable on ancient coins, and should *never* be removed. Such oxidation is called patina. Patina is the thin layer of material that often forms on the surfaces of many bronze coins after long contact with atmosphere, soil, moisture, or other factors. The patina can form in various colors, ranging from red or orange to deep jade green. Ancient bronze or copper coins with a uniform jade-green patina are worth many times more than coins without such patina.

Dr. Arie Kindler, director of Israel's Kadman Numismatic Museum, has written that for the purpose of cleaning, ancient coins may be divided into three main categories:

1. *Worn*—that is, rubbed down so that cleaning would be of no value at all

2. *Covered with a delicate patina*—which, if it does not prevent the reading of the legend or cover the design, would only suffer through cleaning, and, therefore, no such steps should be taken

3. *Covered with a thick layer of dirt and corrosion*—but with the possibility still remaining that cleaning would reveal enough to identify the coin and leave it in reasonable condition

As I have said already, the cleaning of ancient coins, both bronze and silver, is a task best left to the expert conservator in this field.

Nevertheless, it is my experience that collectors of ancient coins will at least once get the urge to buy a corroded and encrusted coin and try to clean it up in the hope it will be of value. I have seen coins cleaned by methods ranging from brushing with an abrasive toothpaste for many hours to tumbling in a stone-polishing machine. These cleaning methods are generally not effective, since they can do more harm than good.

Here is some advice from Dr. Kindler on cleaning ancient coins chemically:

"The solution of the chemical bath consists of one part sulphuric acid to nine parts distilled water. The coin is left in the solution for several hours, by which process the patina is dissolved, as well as the dirt. The coin is then removed from the acid and brushed with a fingernail brush to remove the brown material that has formed on its surface. If dirt still remains on the coin, the process is repeated. If, after the coin has undergone this process four times, it is still not clean, a new solution should be prepared. To remove all traces of the acid, the coin is left in distilled water for two weeks, the water being changed every day. Upon being removed from the distilled water, the coin is to be washed in soap and hot water, no brush being used."

The Coin Plague

To be distinguished from the deep-green, stable patina many ancient bronze coins acquire is the light-green, powdery deposit known as coin plague. This "plague" can grow rapidly over an entire collection of ancient bronze coins, especially if they are not stored properly. The coin plague is caused by humidity combined with harmful substances either on the coin or in the air. I have seen a collection that was supposedly "healthy" only weeks before with a severe case of this "disease."

To prevent the coin plague in the first place, make sure that your coins are kept in a clean, dry place. The coin plague can spread, so if you find the green speckles "growing" on one of your coins, remove it from the rest of the coins immediately.

Here is Dr. Yaakov Meshorer's method of curing a coin of the coin plague.

With a splinter of wood, a toothpick, or a bristle toothbrush, carefully scrape away as much of the green material as possible.

Then begin soaking the coin in a glass of distilled water. In very serious cases you may add a small amount of soap to the water.

Change the water, rinsing the coin and the glass every two days. Keep repeating this process for at least three weeks, even if the plague seems to have disappeared sooner.

When the process is finished, dry the coin with a cloth, then place it under the bulb of a desk lamp for several hours so it becomes thoroughly dry.

You may then spray the coin with a uniform, thin coat of a flat-finish lacquer, which you can buy at an art supply store.

If over a period of time the plague returns to this coin—it should not if you have followed the above instructions carefully—you can remove the lacquer with thinner and repeat the entire process.

This method is effective only if coin plague affects just the surface of a coin. If the plague has penetrated to the core of the coin, it is unlikely that any home-treatment method will save the coin. If this has happened to a particularly valuable coin in your collection, I suggest you contact an archaeology expert from either a local museum or a university for advice on who will be able to help you preserve this coin properly.

12. Detecting Counterfeit Coins

There is hardly an advanced coin collector in the world who can say with a straight face that he has never unwittingly bought an altered or forged coin.

A collection of forgeries of ancient coins of various types.

But more often than not it seems that collectors and dealers catch up with the phonies. Luckily the vast majority of counterfeit and altered coins are quite readily detectable. There are sometimes coins, however, that even the experts cannot agree upon.

Don't be misled into believing that only the rarest and most expensive coins are liable to be counterfeited. I have seen forgeries of coins that even if genuine would sell for only a few dollars.

Before coin collecting became popular, the only reason for the counterfeiter to replicate a coin was to cheat the government or merchants by putting the coin into circulation and thus gaining a particular amount of money. In ancient times, when the designs on coins were only a convenient way to guarantee the weight of metal, forgers were faced with an interesting problem.

If, for example, the forger wanted to make a copy of a silver tetradrachm, he could not make it out of the same quality silver as the actual coin. If he did, what would be the point of his illegal practice? The counterfeiter's solution was to model a coin from a base metal such as copper or pot metal, then plate it thinly with silver or a silverlike substance.

Indeed, many of these ancient forgeries exist today, and they are known as fourée or plated pieces. They are usually lighter than the genuine ancient coins, and most of the time there is a defect in the silver plating so the base metal underneath can be seen. Occasionally an ancient forgery is found with rather large lumps in its fabric. These lumps occur because the bronze or copper core of the coin has started to corrode, thus forcing the silver plating to bulge in this unsightly manner.

The ancient forgeries are of true interest and value to the collector, but they are generally less expensive than a comparable genuine ancient coin. When an ancient coin is known by a dealer to be a fourée, the dealer should describe it as such in any catalogue or listing, since this is a major factor in the coin's description.

Controversial Fakes

As mentioned already, some coins thought to be forgeries are genuinely controversial. It is not unusual for two experts to disagree on whether a particular coin is genuine or not. Once I purchased from a reputable dealer a large bronze coin of Vespasian.

When I showed it to a knowledgeable friend he said he thought it was a forgery.

I then took it to a coin dealer in New York who is said to be one of the world's greatest experts on ancient Roman bronze coins. He, too, said it was a forgery.

The next time I visited Washington, D.C., I showed the coin to one of the ancient-coin curators at the Smithsonian Institution. He said it was genuine!

By this time I was no longer sure of anything. I decided to seek the best available advice on ancient coins—from the experts at the British Museum. I had the coin sent to a dealer friend in London, who carried it to one of the British Museum's experts. The report came back that the coin had been carefully examined, and it was believed to be genuine.

"The coin does have a slightly cast appearance," the British Museum expert said, "but this is probably due to the fact that it seems to have been one of the coins found at the bottom of the River Tiber."

Many years ago, a supposed numismatic "expert" viewed my father's collection of ancient coins of Bible days. One of the coins on display was a replica of an ancient shekel.

The expert said he was sure that this coin was genuine, and offered to pay several hundred dollars for it. My father, knowing it was a replica, refused to sell.

Many dealers have stories to tell of rare coins or medals they have sold, only to have them returned by collectors who believe they are forgeries. Often the dealers believe these coins to be genuine and send them to the American Numismatic Association Certification Service, where they are, indeed, sometimes found to be genuine. Sometimes, of course, they are not found to be genuine, and then reputable dealers have an obligation to remove them from sale permanently. More than one dealer has purchased coins only to find that some or all of them are counterfeits and cannot be resold.

Virtually every type of coin has been forged or counterfeited, from the oldest ancient coins to foreign coins and United States cents.

Unfortunately I have no magical formula or profound words of wisdom that will help you spot counterfeits in any situation. While I do not feel it is terribly difficult to detect counterfeit coins in most instances, the ability to do this will depend on your own knowledge.

Friends who are beginners or noncollectors will often ask me how I know a particular coin is not counterfeit. Although inadequate, my most frequent reply is, "I just know it."

The experienced numismatist can literally feel and see a counterfeit coin. Such a reaction may be triggered by any number of factors, some of which are completely unknown to the novice. Later in this chapter I'll discuss a number of them.

Altered Coins

Often counterfeiters will try to alter genuine coins to make them seem more rare or more desirable to the collector. In spite of the fact that such coins began as genuine pieces, they should also be considered counterfeit, since they are not genuine products of the mint.

Tooling is especially common in larger ancient bronze coins, but many ancient coins have been carefully tooled to raise the relief of the design or even to change the legend altogether. On the other hand, sometimes an ancient coin is "tooled" simply to remove encrustation or patina, and the actual metal of the coin is not really touched.

United States coins are often altered by counterfeiters to make them more desirable. Mint marks can be removed, added, and changed. Dates can also be tampered with.

A mint mark can be shaved away altogether and replaced by another one taken from a similar coin. It may be soldered or glued into place. Sometimes a drop of silver solder can be put into a number such as an O and then it can be recarved to look like a 3. Sometimes a mint mark can be added by a special punch, and then the traces of the punch itself are carefully removed so the mint mark appears to be raised above the coin's field.

Thus you should carefully examine the mint mark and date of any coins you might purchase, especially rare or unusual dates or mints.

Another trick of the counterfeiter is to shave down two common coins, such as a plain obverse and a mint marked reverse. Then the two halves can be soldered together. If the forger wants to do this to a reeded-edge coin he can hollow out the obverse or reverse and insert the shaved-down portion from another coin. If the work is done carefully the rim blends almost perfectly with the seam.

Using some of these coin-altering techniques, the skilled counterfeiter can transform the relatively inexpensive 1909-VDB into a coin worth several hundred dollars by adding a tiny "S" mint mark.

The relatively common 1944-D cent can be altered by the skilled counterfeiter to seem to be a rare 1914-D cent.

Also beware of:

- 1858 cents altered so they seem to be 1856 cents
- 1919-S cents altered to seem to be 1909-S cents
- 1922-D cents altered to appear to be 1922-P cents
- 1948 P,D,S cents (copper) altered to appear to be 1943 P,D,S cents
- 1910 nickels altered to seem to be 1913 nickels
- 1956 or 1959-D nickels altered to appear to be 1950-D nickels
- 1924 P,D dimes altered to appear to be 1921 P,D dimes
- 1934-D dimes altered to appear to be 1931-D dimes
- 1942 dimes altered to appear to be 1942/1 dimes
- 1928 quarters altered to appear to be 1923-S quarters
- 1932-P quarters altered to seem to be 1932-D,S quarters

These are just a few of the possibilities that clever counterfeiters use to prey upon unsuspecting collectors.

If you are an error collector you must also beware of forgeries, since there are many methods to produce "error" coins that may seem genuine to the untrained collector's eye.

Types of Forgeries

The three most common types of forged coins are produced by one of three methods: casting, striking, or electroplating.

By far the most common forgeries—because they are the easiest to produce—are the casts. The vast majority of modern and ancient coins have been struck by dies, and thus any cast coin should immediately come under suspicion.

Here are a few methods you can use to determine whether a coin has been cast:

- Often cast coins have an especially soft "greasy" feel to them, especially when they have been made of base metal.
- Base-metal pieces that have been plated will have lost a good deal of definition because of the thickness of the plating material.
- Since cast coins are often cast in sand or plaster molds, they often have a slightly gritty appearance. This is usually most pronounced in the finely detailed areas of the coin.
- Cast coins invariably show less detail and definition than the originals, even if they are molded from casts of uncirculated or proof coins.
- Cast coins will have a seam mark along the edge of the coin where the two halves of the mold were joined together. Counterfeiters go to extreme lengths to file and buff, but portions of the seams—or filemarks—invariably remain.
- If the coin has a reeded edge, examine it carefully. Genuine reeded edges are usually uniform in length, width, depth, and direction. Counterfeits often show a lack of this uniformity.
- If it is possible to drop the coin from a few inches onto a solid surface, such as a heavy wood desktop, it should ring with full pitch. Dull rings or thuds often indicate cast forgeries.
- Cast coins almost always have characteristic pits or pocks, which result from tiny bubbles in the molten metal. These

can be reduced and almost eliminated by use of pressure casting techniques.

• Weigh the coin. Official weights and tolerances for all United States coins, and many foreign pieces, are readily available. Coins should fall within a small tolerance range for all specifications. Here is a list of the weights, in grains, for most United States coins.

Denomination	Dates	Weight (grains)
Half Cent	1793–1795	104.00
Half Cent	1796–1857	84.00
Large Cent	1793–1795	208.00
Large Cent	1796–1857	168.00
Small Cent	1856–1864	72.00
Small Cent	1864–1942	48.00
Small Cent	1943	42.50
Small Cent	1944–	48.00
Two Cent	1864–1873	96.00
Three Cent (nickel)	1865–1889	30.00
Three Cent (silver)	1851–1853	12.38
Three Cent (silver)	1854–1873	11.52
Five Cent (nickel)	1866–1942	77.16
Five Cent (silver)	1942–1945	77.16
Five Cent (nickel)	1946–	77.16
Half Dime	1794–1837	20.80
Half Dime	1837–1853	20.63
Half Dime	1853–1873	19.20
Dime	1796–1837	41.60
Dime	1837–1853	41.25
Dime	1853–1873	38.40
Dime	1873–1964	38.58
Dime	1965–	35.00
Twenty Cent	1875–1878	77.16
Quarter	1796–1836	104.00
Quarter	1837–1852	103.13
Quarter	1853–1873	96.00
Quarter	1873–1964	96.45
Quarter	1965–	87.50
Half Dollar	1794–1836	208.00
Half Dollar	1837–1852	206.25
Half Dollar	1853–1873	192.00

Half Dollar	1873–1964	192.90
Half Dollar	1965–	177.50
Silver Dollar	1794–1803	416.00
Silver Dollar	1836–1935	412.50
Silver Dollar (clad)	1971–	350.00
Silver Dollar (silver-clad)	1971–	379.50
Trade Dollar	1873–1883	420.00
Gold Dollar	1849–1889	25.80
Gold Quarter Eagle	1796–1834	67.50
Gold Quarter Eagle	1834–1929	64.50
Gold Three Dollar	1854–1889	77.40
Gold Four Dollar	1879–1880	108.00
Gold Half Eagle	1795–1834	135.00
Gold Half Eagle	1834–1929	129.00
Gold Eagle	1795–1804	270.00
Gold Eagle	1838–1933	258.00
Gold Double Eagle	1850–1933	516.00
Gold Fifty Dollar	1915	1,290.00

Die-struck forgeries are often more difficult to detect than their cast counterparts. But they are most often given away by the style of the engraving, weight of the coin, and comparison with known die varieties of the same coin. Die-struck forgeries may also carry concentric rings on their surfaces, which result from the reproduction of the genuine piece with a tracing tool. Also, die-struck forgeries may show more detail at the center than at the edges.

An electroplate forgery which has been broken apart to show the thin shell and the base-metal interior.

Electrotypes were originally used by museums to duplicate coins for study by students of ancient history and numismatics. They are very close indeed to the coins from which they were copied. But the electrotype consists of a shell of the coin's obverse, and one of the reverse, filled with a base metal for weight and joined by an edge seam. Some people began to alter these coins to make them appear to be genuine, by filing down the edges and re-plating them. Some of them have found their way into collections, and the museums stopped making them some years ago.

Detecting Ancient Forgeries

Here are some detection methods for forgeries of ancient coins:

- Examine the coin for general appearance to the naked eye. Does it appear to be ancient? Does the coin have a cast look?
- Examine the coin with a good magnifying glass. Do the edges show any filemarks or seams? Is the surface of the coin covered with casting pockmarks?

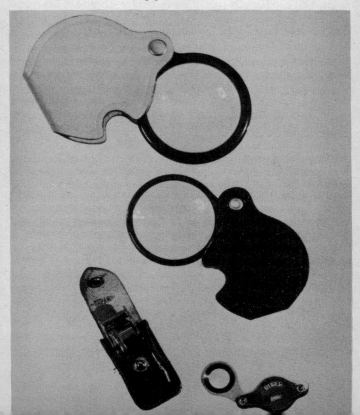

- Does the legend show any sign of alteration or tooling?
- Does the patina on a bronze coin appear to be genuine? Remember, though, that large numbers of ancient bronze coins are found in a condition that requires cleaning and eventual retoning of the coin. Some collectors refuse to buy ancient coins that have been cleaned. Such coins are acceptable to me as long as they have been cleaned skillfully and lightly, and the coins themselves have not been altered.
- Is the coin of the correct size and weight? Frequently forgeries will be considerably heavier or lighter than specimens of the same coin known to be genuine.

It is well worth noting that any coins—modern or ancient—can be genuine and yet have certain characteristics of counterfeit coins. This is especially true of coins that have been heavily worn or mishandled in some way. Don't be hasty in decisions, but bring questionable material to the attention of an expert.

The Best Precaution

Other than becoming an expert yourself, the best possible precaution is to purchase coins from reputable dealers who stand behind the material they sell.

If you are not satisfied that a coin is authentic, check it with an expert in the field. The extra effort will be well worth your while.

There should be no "time limit" on any guarantee of a coin's genuineness. A dealer who sells a coin through the mail, for example, may have a seven-day period during which you can return a coin for any reason. This allows you to see a coin with your own eyes before finally buying it. But if you should discover a month, a year, or more later that the coin is a forgery, you should be able to return it for a full refund, *as long as you retain the receipt and can show it is the same coin you purchased originally.*

ANACS

The American Numismatic Association maintains a certification service (ANACS) in Colorado Springs, Colo. You can send the ANACS a coin which you may want to have authenticated. The ANACS, according to its advertisements:

- Renders an opinion as to whether a coin is genuine or otherwise.

- Issues a photo certificate with a registered number on genuine coins. It is returned with the coin.
- Returns most modern issue coins within a few working days. Other specialized coins take somewhat longer.
- Cannot: Grade, attribute, or do valuations of coins.

Collectors who want to take advantage of this ANACS service should send their coins to ANACS, 818 N. Cascade, Colorado Springs, CO 80903.

The current ANACS fee schedule is as follows:

Owner's value	ANACS base fee	ANA member fee
$ 0-125	$6.00	$5.40
$126-250	$9.00	$8.10
$251-375	$12.00	$10.80
$376-500	$15.00	$13.50
over $500	3% of value	2.7% of value
Maximum base fee: $500		

13. Protecting Your Coin Collection

Mishandling and improperly storing coins are among the most common errors made by beginning coin collectors. You must learn to keep your coins in the best possible condition. A collection of modern or ancient coins or medals worth many thousands of dollars can be made next to worthless if it is not taken care of properly. What a shame it is when a coin that has been beautifully preserved for many years is carelessly handled and spoiled.

When you handle your coins, the most important thing to remember is to move slowly—don't grab. At coin shows I have seen eager collectors grab for coins held by a dealer or another collector. In their haste they have knocked coins to the table or floor. Valuable coins have been lost or irreparably damaged by scratches or nicks acquired in such accidents. Hold coins over a pad or other soft surface as insurance.

Always grip coins by their edges. Make sure your hands are free of moisture, or any other foreign substances. *Never* put your fingers on the obverse or reverse of a coin. Even if you think your fingers are clean and dry, they carry traces of grease, salts, and other chemicals. You may not even notice a fingerprint right after placing your thumb or finger on the surface of a proof or BU coin. But put that coin away for a while and the finger marks will become increasingly visible as time passes, marking the coin with an indelible "stain" that decreases its beauty and value forever.

If you handle a lot of BU coins or medals, mint sets, or proof sets, you will want to invest in a few dollars in an inexpensive pair of white cotton gloves. Your family and friends might tease you when they see you donning white gloves to handle some of your precious coins, but you will know that you are protecting your investment.

Coin Dangers

The major factors to consider in storing your coin collection are protection from atmospheric elements, protection from other physical damage, and convenience and availability. Of course, protection from theft is a very important consideration, and I will devote a section at the end of this chapter exclusively to that problem.

The atmospheric elements most dangerous to your coins are chemical fumes and water vapor. They can cause changes in your coins ranging from minor discoloration to severe corrosion spots. Thus be sure to find a clean and dry place to keep your coin collection.

If you keep your coins in a closed space such as a filing cabinet, safety deposit box, or safe, you should consider using one of the chemical desiccants to keep the air free of moisture. These must not be used in open spaces, since they will quickly absorb their limit and be valueless. The best desiccant is indicator-type silica gel. Try to buy a large container of these crystals, which start off blue and white in color. As they absorb moisture they slowly turn pink, and no blue remains when the saturation point has been reached. Then you must change the supply of silica gel. The "used" material can be recycled by drying it out in the oven for an hour or so. Keep the gel in a cloth bag and check it every few weeks or so to see if a change is needed.

Coin Storage

You will probably spend hours deciding which method of coin storage best suits your collection and your circumstances. You want an attractive, convenient storage method that gives maximum protection to your coins. If you are like most coin collectors —myself included—you will change your method of coin storage many times before you settle on one.

The classic method of coin storage is the *coin cabinet*. In Europe several hundred years ago, these elegant pieces of furniture were an important part of every well-to-do household. Security being what it is today, however, most collectors do not want to keep their coins in a cabinet at home.

Nevertheless, an antique coin cabinet can be a fine piece of furniture in which you can store inexpensive but interesting coins, tokens, and medals; photographic cutouts of your actual coin collection; plaster casts of your coins (especially if you collect ancients); or even reproductions of valuable coins.

Coin cabinets are often ornate and beautifully made, with a number of flat drawers, each drawer having a number of cutouts or depressions to hold individual coins.

Coin trays are especially popular with collectors of ancient coins, since these specimens can be more safely handled than modern coins, especially modern uncirculated and proof specimens. Trays today are most frequently made of combinations of wood, cloth, and plastic, and several trays fit snugly in a special carrying case. Each tray has compartments for a number of coins, and many collectors like to keep a thin cardboard disc with each coin. On this disc you can write identification information.

If you want to store your coins in trays, but can't find any for sale through coin dealers, check with a local jeweler to see if he knows of similar trays made for small jewelry stock storage.

Although coin cabinets and coin trays are among the most elegant methods of storing your coins, the vast majority of collectors will choose one of the following methods, which is generally more convenient.

Coin folders are one of the least expensive methods of storing your collection. These heavy cardboard folders are ready-made to accept various series of coins ranging from Lincoln cents to type collections and dozens of others. The folders have holes into which the coins specified will snugly fit, and they are simply pushed into place. This is the method most beginning collectors will use, and folders are quite satisfactory, especially if most of the coins in your collection are being taken from circulation.

Coin folders also have their disadvantages. Often coins must be pushed and prodded to fit into the precut holes, and often coins don't fit snugly enough and they repeatedly fall out. If the coins are put into the folders once, and never removed, falling out is not usually a problem, but then, unfortunately, only one side of the coin is visible.

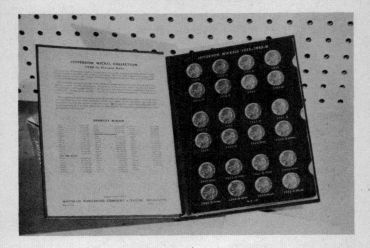

Coin albums are another popular method of storing coins. They can come in complete units of several pages, much the same size as the coin folders, or in ring-bound albums with loose-leaf pages. The more expensive albums, like the folders, are made of heavy cardboard and have holes die-cut for particular coins. The holes in the pages of the coin albums, however, are punched all the way through, and strips of clear plastic slide across horizontal rows,

protecting the coins but allowing them to be viewed from both the front and the back without removing them. Coins cannot fall out of these albums either. But care must be taken that you do not continually rub the plastic strips against the coins as the strips are slid in and out.

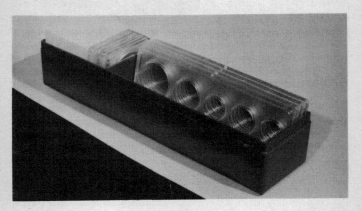

Plastic coin holders are usually made of Lucite or similar new plastics, and will hold one coin or a relatively small set of coins. These are rather an expensive way to store your coins, and not convenient if you have a very large collection. Holes are made in the plastic base and a top plate is screwed onto it. Both the obverse and reverse of coins can be seen without removing them, and they are quite secure against other damage. These coin holders are relatively expensive, but they are just right to display that special set of coins you are very proud of.

Individual coin envelopes are a convenient and inexpensive method of storing your coins. Many "purists" swear that this is the only safe way to store your coins. The coin envelopes are usually made of brown paper, but are also available in colors. They are usually 2 × 2 inches square, with a single flap that is not gummed. Larger and smaller sizes are also made, but may be more difficult to find.

These envelopes should be made of paper that is "neutral" to your coins. (Some paper stocks and glues are high in acids or other chemicals and could damage coins stored in them over a period of months or years.)

Another advantage of these paper envelopes is that their surfaces allow plenty of room to describe the coin inside, and details about its purchase.

Many collectors like to give additional protection to their coins by first placing them in cellophane, glassine, or polyethylene sleeves, and then putting them in the paper envelopes. This is very good insurance, especially for your valuable uncirculated and proof coins. The sleeves are made in several sizes and can be matched closely with the coins, whether they are cents or silver dollars.

Some other collectors like to keep their coins in these *plastic sleeves* alone. You can do this by putting the coin in a sleeve of the proper size, making a few folds of about ¼ inch each at the open end of the sleeve, and fastening this with a staple to a 2 × 2-inch-square card cut from white card stock. Write the identification information on the card.

The advantage of this method is that you can view both sides of the coin by simply flipping the envelope back, while with the paper envelopes you must remove the coin before viewing it. Purists, on the other hand, don't like to use staples in displaying their coins, since their sharp edges are a potential hazard to both the neatness of the display and the condition of the coin. Also, staples will discolor and rust over a few years time.

Cardboard and cellophane holders, 2 × 2 inches square, are another coin storage method used by many collectors. They have precut holes of various sizes, covered with cellophane. The coin is inserted between the folded halves of this type of holder, and then it is taped or stapled closed. Identifying information can be written on the cardboard, and both sides of the coin are visible without removing it.

Rapidly increasing in popularity are *plastic flip envelopes*, made of clear vinyl. Flips are commonly found in the 2 × 2-inch size, but are also available in smaller and larger sizes. Each flip consists basically of two plastic pockets. Into one pocket goes the coin, and into the other a piece of thin cardboard or paper with your identification information. Flips allow you to see both sides of the coin with a minimum amount of effort, and they are reusable.

Most coin dealers also carry specially made plastic loose-leaf notebook pages, with several rows of pockets. Pages are available for all of the standard-size flips or cardboard holders.

If you decide to keep your coins in any of the individual storage holders—envelopes, holders, or flips—you may also want to consider cardboard, plastic, or metal storage boxes. These boxes are also available for all of the standard sizes, and are especially con-

venient if you have a large collection and want to keep it in the smallest possible space.

Many collectors have discovered that their 2 × 2-inch coin holders fit perfectly in any of the number of trays or carrying cases originally made for 2×2-inch film transparencies. Today many slide photographers store their slides in automatic cassettes or cartridges, so the older sturdy metal trays are often available at very low cost. You may ask for them at your local camera-supply store, but they will just as likely be found in the basement of a longtime photographer, or for 50 cents or so at a local flea market or garage sale.

If you have obtained rolls of coins for collecting or investment purposes you will also want to consider the best storage method. Special plastic tubes are made in sizes for all denominations of United States coins, and a few odd sizes as well. These tubes are excellent protection for your coin rolls.

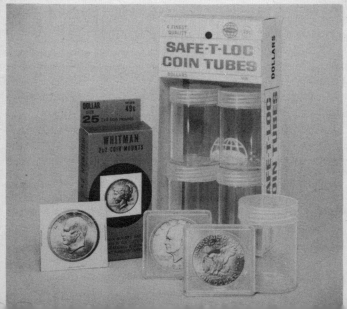

Guarding Against Theft

Your concern about the theft of your collection is, of course, related to its value. If you are a beginning collector who has only a few dozen inexpensive coins, you will probably want to keep your collection right at home.

But as your collection grows in size and value you will begin to consider security a major problem. One of the easiest methods of solving the security problem is to rent a safety deposit box at a nearby bank. These are available in several sizes, and often cost less than $20 per year—a small price indeed to pay for the safety of a valuable collection! Unfortunately, as safe as this storage method might be, it also has disadvantages. The major one is the problem of "visiting hours." If you are an avid collector, you will want to look at your coins frequently, and show them to friends. If they are kept in a bank box, this is very inconvenient.

If you have a large coin collection and do not want to keep it in a safety deposit box, you can obtain various security devices for your home, ranging from safes to complicated electronic alarm devices.

Incidentally, it is also well worth your while at this time to make sure the locks on all of the doors and windows to your home are secure. Your locksmith will probably be able to tell you about the various kinds of home safes that are available.

Here are some other security tips:

- •Don't freely talk and brag about your coin collection and its value, especially to people you don't know.
- •When talking about your coin collection, make it a point to state that it is kept in a bank box and not at home.
- •If you exhibit your collection anywhere, don't distribute business cards or other information with the address of where the collection is stored.
- •If you have coins when traveling, use the hotel safe to store them.
- •Do not receive any of your numismatic mail at home. Rent a nearby post office box for only a few dollars a year.
- •Very rare and valuable items should be kept away from the bulk of your collection.
- •If you have had a lot of publicity over your coin collection, and it is well known, you might want to consider an unlisted telephone number. With this protection, a potential thief

cannot obtain your address from the operator or the phone book, nor can he telephone your house to see whether you are at home.
• Coin collection insurance can be obtained at a nominal cost through the American Numismatic Association. If you want to insure the collection privately, check with your insurance broker.

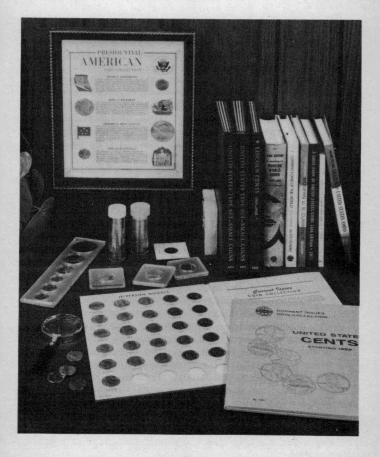

14. Buying and Selling Coins

The keys to your success in buying coins for your collection—and eventually selling them at a profit—are essentially two: your own knowledge and the dealers from whom you buy.

Many have put forth their criteria for evaluating coin dealers. Since I have been a collector of coins for more than 20 years, I have come to some of my own conclusions. But before discussing them let me quote my friend Joe Rose, president of Harmer Rooke Numismatics in New York. Joe always tells both coin collectors and investors to follow a few rules about collecting. "If you're putting money into something, learn about it. You wouldn't buy into the stock market without any knowledge on the word of somebody you didn't know," he says.

Rose adds his opinion that "no dealer, I don't care who he is, has any right to expect exclusivity from a customer. The dealer is not going to have the customer forever. When a customer comes to me, I don't care who else he buys from. I want to give him the best deal possible."

Now let me give you my tips on finding and doing business with coin dealers.

Buy from dealers who are members of numismatic organizations. Some of the organizations are especially for dealers, such as the Professional Numismatists Guild and the International Association of Professional Numismatists. But these are primarily for larger dealers, and some of the most knowledgeable and honest coin dealers in the United States *are not* members of these groups. Such dealers are, however, members of the American Numismatic Association, the American Israel Numismatic Association, the Token and Medals Society, and many other fine groups of numismatists. All of the good collectors' and dealers' organizations will move quickly to prevent unscrupulous persons from taking advantage of their good names, or the trust of their members. If you are a member of a coin club you should encourage such actions when warranted.

The size of a coin dealer may not mean much. In other words,

you will be able to find just as many—maybe more—"buys" from the small dealers as you can from the larger ones. Indeed, the smaller dealers frequently have much smaller overhead and operating expenses and therefore can sell at lower prices. On the other hand, larger dealers may sometimes offer a larger range of stock and services to their customers.

Make sure that the dealers you buy from are knowledgeable. Coin dealers whom you patronize should complement your knowledge, and even act as your guide and teacher in numismatics.

Never buy a coin from a dealer who tells you it is being sold "as is" or is "not returnable." All coins should be subject to your inspection and return, especially if you later find them to be unfairly described or altered in any way not originally disclosed. Do not, however, be unreasonable in your desire for a return privilege. Most dealers who sell coins by mail, for example, allow a week-long return privilege for any reason. This time will allow you to examine each coin and make sure it satisfies you. The only reason you should ask to make a return after this time has elapsed is if the coin's authenticity or ownership is seriously called into question.

In his famous laws of ecology, Dr. Barry Commoner has proclaimed, "There is no such thing as a free lunch." This is also good advice for coin collectors. Santa Claus does not exist in this field. Beware of coins that are priced "unbelievably low." Rarely you will find a legitimate coin priced in this way, especially if it is an extreme rarity in an obscure specialty field. Overall, however, coins which appear to be "too cheap" may be fake, overgraded, altered, or even stolen merchandise.

Don't be too quick to condemn a coin dealer for what may be a legitimate mistake. Anyone who has spent many consecutive hours and days identifying, grading, and cataloguing numismatic material can vouch for the fact that it is not difficult to make errors under such circumstances. If a dealer has made an error with regard to grading or attributing a coin he has sold you, give the dealer a chance to rectify the error. He should immediately refund your money or, if possible and you desire it, replace the merchandise with material that is satisfactory. By the way, I am not overly fond of those dealers who do not offer to refund purchase price, but say "exchanges only." That's not cricket.

If a dealer repeatedly makes errors in filling your orders, you would be wise to steer yourself to another dealer.

If you have a major problem with a coin dealer, and you cannot get satisfaction, do not hesitate to report the matter to any publications in which he advertises, the major coin clubs, and any law-enforcement agencies which may be involved. If a coin dealer defrauds you, for example, you should report him to the local law-enforcement authorities. If a coin dealer solicits your business through the mail and then cheats you in some way, bring the case to the attention of federal postal authorities, who will investigate the matter to see if postal fraud has occurred. (Incidentally, collectors who buy through the mail are also subject to the same laws. If a collector orders coins which are delivered to him, the collector must pay for the coins within the time limits specified, or return them.)

Fortunately most collectors and dealers in the field of numismatics are honest. Here are a few more points you ought to keep in mind to ensure that your relationships with coin dealers will result in mutual advantage and satisfaction.

No matter whom you buy from or where, make sure you get a bill that specifies the date and type of coin, mint mark, condition, defects, etc. When you have such a document you will be protected in case any question over a particular coin arises.

Remember that a dealer is in business to make money. This holds true for both full-time and part-time dealers. You may choose to invest your money in stocks, bonds, or bank accounts. The coin dealer invests in his stock of merchandise. He is entitled to have a fair return on his investment as well as to be paid for his time and efforts on your behalf.

Thus the coin dealer will sell coins for more than he pays for them. The markup for better-grade United States coins, for example, generally runs about 35 percent. Thus if you were to purchase a coin with a fair retail market value of $100 and take it to a coin dealer to sell, he should offer you approximately $70 for the coin.

This price structure does not hold as true for ancient coins, since the market is much broader and the coins much more rare. Thus there are not any frequently published pricing standards such as with United States coins and certain foreign coins.

The 35 percent rule of thumb is also invalid if the coins involved are in average or poor condition, very common, or otherwise not very desirable. In such cases the dealer may require a much higher return, since he will have to hold the coins for a very long time. On the other hand, markups of 10 percent or even less are not uncommon in the coin business if the coins involved are likely to be sold quickly.

When trading with a coin dealer remember that the trade may be a bit of recreation for you, but it is business for the dealer. Of course you can haggle, and can expect some reasonable give and take on terms. However, to stay in business the dealer must make money on his transactions. That is, he must make his profit both on the coin he is "selling" to you and on his future sale of the coin you trade to him. This is the same thing any dealer would expect if he sold you a coin and then used the money you paid him to buy another coin, which he would later resell at a profit. We don't mean to discourage collectors from offering trades to dealers, since many dealers enjoy doing business in this way. But for some reason, many collectors think dealers can afford to make trades without profit, while requiring profit in all of their other transactions.

Don't treat coin dealers unfairly. If a dealer mails you a coin and you decide to return it, do it promptly. There is very likely another collector waiting to see it, and to tie up the dealer's stock in this way is simply unfair. Every dealer who deals through the mails expects a reasonable number of coins to be returned—approval buying, after all, means just that.

On the other hand, most dealers have "black lists" of customers who are chronic returners. If you are one of them, don't be surprised if the coin dealers are not so quick to fill your orders or requests for coins on approval in the future.

Pay your bills promptly. Don't expect a coin dealer to "carry" you on a bill unless you have made advance arrangements. Most coin dealers simply cannot afford to give you this kind of service, and the price you were charged for a coin did not take into account the possibility that you might not pay your bill for many weeks. So pay on time. You would expect as much.

Buying by Mail

If you turn to the advertising pages of any of the numismatic periodicals as well as many national publications, you will find advertisements by dealers who will send you catalogues through the mail. Many such catalogues are free; others cost a nominal sum, and are usually well worth the money.

Buying coins in the relaxed atmosphere of your own home is a fine way to collect. You can carefully examine coins that are offered to you without the pressure of a "sales pitch."

Many collectors also enjoy the pace of buying through the mail —one or two coins at a time several times each year. Indeed, this is the only way for coin collectors in many small towns or isolated communities to add to their collections. Many fine friendships have developed between collectors and dealers who have done business with each other through the mails for many years.

You will probably receive your coins via insured or registered mail. Insured mail will cover values of up to only $200; mail worth more than that must be sent registered if it is to be covered by the United States Post Office insurance system.

Today both insured and registered mail can be sent *first class*. Once insured mail could only be sent by third class or airmail.

Nevertheless, insured packets can take two or more weeks to arrive at their destinations, although they may do so more quickly. Registered packets seem to arrive more quickly—although registered mail is quite a bit more expensive. As a general rule it is your responsibility to pay the postage *both ways* on coins you request and then return. Some dealers will pay the postage to you if your purchases exceed a given amount, such as $25.

Remember, once you have signed for a coin that has been delivered to you by mail, it is your responsibility until it is safely returned to the dealer. If you deface or damage the coin in any way you can be legally expected to pay for it. Handle with *extreme* care.

When you return coins to a dealer you should, first of all, be sure they are well protected for mailing. Most coin dealers can supply you with special coin mailers. Wrap the coin carefully in tissue, then in cardboard, it you don't have any mailers. When you mail the coins be sure to register or insure them for the full amount of their value, since you are responsible for the full retail value of the merchandise until the dealer has it back. Be sure to keep the postal receipts for any packages you might send, since this is your only proof that the material was sent insured.

Coin Auctions

Many collectors are frightened away by coin auctions. This is really a shame, since I can't think of any more exciting—and often economical—way to buy coins. With a few precautions you should feel free to bid in both floor auctions and mail-bid auctions.

In floor auctions you should:

- First read the "terms of sale" which will be found at the front of the auction catalogue. Is it an "unreserved" sale, or are there bidding floors for certain items? Are all items guaranteed to be genuine and as described? If not, think twice before buying questionable items. Do you understand the terms for payment and delivery?
- Be sure to examine coins before the sale, since coins bought by bidders on the floor are not usually subject to return.
- Make sure the auctioneer knows when you are bidding on an item—or when you are not bidding on it! Don't hesitate to ask a question if you are uncertain about the stage of the bidding or the high bidder at a specific point.
- Pay attention at all times. Keep your hands down unless you are bidding.
- Inspect merchandise before paying for it to make sure it has not been damaged since you inspected it prior to the sale.

In mail-bid auctions you should:

- •First read the "terms of sale," which will be found at the front of the auction catalogue. Ask the same kinds of questions you would ask regarding a floor-bid auction. You should also make sure that coins are returnable if you do not feel they are up to their descriptions. This should hold true even for coins which have been photographed in the catalogue, since a picture can often look different from the coin itself.
- •Find out what kind of arrangement is made by the auctioneer for mail bidders. Usually you can expect the auctioneer to buy a lot for you at the lowest possible price. This is usually one step (generally 10 percent) above the second-highest bidder. Thus if there is a coin you want very badly and you bid $100 for it, you should get it for $27.50 if the second-highest bidder submitted a bid for $25. Some mail-bid auctions do not work in this way, so it is best to find out in advance.
- •Find out whether you will be charged a commission when your bid is executed. Such commissions are not common in the United States, but are the rule in numismatic auctions in Europe and Israel.
- •Do not make ridiculously low bids. Generally it is not worth your while to bid less than half of the estimate for a particular lot. In some auctions the catalogues will specifically state the minimum acceptable bid.
- •Do not accept coins that do not come up to the description and standards described in the catalogue.

Appendix I
Some Common Numismatic Abbreviations

Note: Abbreviations for coin conditions are listed in Chapter 9.

AE—Latin *aes*—bronze

AR—Latin *argentum*—silver

AU—Latin *aurum*—gold

bil—billon

c.—Latin *circa*—approximately

cf.—Latin *confer*—compare

clnd.—cleaned

cmk.—countermark

c/s—counterstamp

ex.—exergue

mm—millimeter

obv.—obverse

o.c. or o/c—off center

POR—price on request

R—rare

RR—very rare

RRR—extremely rare

RRRR—only one or two specimens known

rev. or rx.—reverse

std.—seated

stg.—standing

Appendix II
Short Numismatic Glossary

ancient coin—usually any coin issued before 500 A.D.

assay—any test to determine the precious-metal content of a coin or other piece of metal

billon—base metal, usually silver and copper

brockage—a coin that has been misstruck so the obverse is struck in incuse on the reverse, or vice versa

bullion—silver or gold in bars or ingots; "bullion value" refers to the metal value of a coin

cabinet friction—slight wear on the surface of a coin caused by rubbing against the tray or envelope in which it is stored

chopmark—a kind of counterstamp made on a coin by an oriental merchant to indicate that he accepted it for full weight and purity; often found on U.S. trade dollars from 1873 to 1878

clipped—coins that have been trimmed on the edges to illegally steal away small amounts of precious metal

countermark—a mark or design struck on a coin to further identify it by changing denomination or legal nation of issue

device—the main elements of design on the obverse and reverse of a coin

epigraphy—the study of inscriptions

field—flat area of a coin between the design and the edge

fourée—ancient forgery of base metal plated with silver

exergue—lower section of a coin's reverse, usually separated from the field by a line

exonumist—one who collects numismatic items aside from those issued for official monetary purposes, such as tokens, medals, scrip, etc.

flan—also "planchet"; the blank upon which a coin, token, or medal is struck

hybrid—coin that was struck with the obverse of one coin type and the reverse of another

incuse—the design struck on a coin in a concave manner

medal—a piece of metal struck or cast to commemorate people or historical events

mule—see **hybrid**

overstrike—coin minted upon a previously struck coin

patina—a natural "skin" that develops over the years, mostly on bronze and copper coins, as a result of oxidation

pattern—a trial strike to test a design or style of coinage

pierced—a coin with a hole drilled or punched in it

restrike—a coin struck from original dies, but later than the original date of issue

retrograde—inscription that is backward (in mirror writing)

token—a coinlike piece, not issued as legal tender

toning—natural coloring of a coin that takes place over a period of time and generally enhances the coin's value

tooled—coin that has been re-engraved to enhance detail or change it altogether

Appendix III
Some Numismatic Publications

COINage
16001 Ventura Blvd.
Encino, CA 91316

Coins Magazine
Iola, WI 54945

Coin World
Box 150
Sidney, OH 45365

Numismatic News
Iola, WI 54945

The Numismatist
American Numismatic
  Association
P.O. Box 2366
Colorado Springs, CO 80901

World Coin News
Iola, WI 54945

Appendix IV
Some Numismatic Organizations
[for Collectors and Dealers]

American Numismatic Association (ANA)
P.O. Box 2366
Colorado Springs, CO 80901

American Israel Numismatic Association (AINA)
91-31 Queens Blvd.
Elmhurst, NY 11373

American Numismatic Society (ANS)
Broadway between 155th and 156th Streets
New York, NY 10032

Canadian Numismatic Association (CNA)
P.O. Box 226
Barrie, Ontario
Canada

International Association of Professional Numismatists (IAPN)
49 Rue de Richelieu
7500 1, Paris
France

Professional Numismatists Guild (PNG)
P.O. Box 371
Courtland, KA 66939

Sociedad Numismatics de Mexico
Apartado Postal 60-589
Mexico, D.F.
Mexico

Index